ISBN:
978-1-906669-02-7

Library of Congress subject heading:
Humor

Published by LDB Publishing

www.chriswoodbooks.co.uk

Cover by www.marcellinodesign.com

Sherlock Holmes

and the

Flying Zombie
Death Monkeys

Chris Wood

LDB Publishing

Manchester

Contents

Sherlock Holmes and the

Flying Zombie Death Monkeys

The door of our Baker Street consulting rooms flew open, and a mature gentleman of dignified aspect rushed in. He was a psychiatrist of some repute, for I recognised him from the press.

"Mr. Holmes, I need your help most urgently." I eyed him with a modicum of pity, for those in direst need who rely on Holmes for assistance are, generally speaking, screwed.

He settled himself down with some agitation, clearly unsettled.

"Please speak freely," Holmes began. "You may talk with absolute confidence."

Our flustered visitor coughed and began with his tale.

"I am Dr. Filbert, one of England's leading psychiatrists, or couch monkeys, if you will. It is my proud boast to have assisted many of the great and the good in their moments of difficulty."

Holmes extended his hand. It was a pleasure for him to meet with someone in a progressive occupation.

"A signal honour to meet you, sir. You and I are pioneers in our respective fields," he purred, as I hid the Napoleon outfits and kicked the foam mallet and rubber chicken into a corner.

"It is my pleasure, but I think we have met before when I had the good fortune to receive your counsel on another singular matter. Sadly, I am in need of your help again."

I shot him a look of commiseration. Life can be very cruel.

"Forgive me for rushing in with such impetuosity, but I have gravest news of matters in government. I particularly apologise to you, sir," here he nodded towards me, "as I realise that conventionally you spend the introductory narrative discussing what a twat Holmes is."

"It cannot be helped," I owned, with a generosity that became me well. "I realise a matter of great momentum is at hand.

Besides," I offered reasonably, "I can always consider what a twat he is afterwards."

"Splendid," agreed he, ignoring Holmes' consternation. "In return for this thoughtful accommodation, I should like to present you with this."

He reached into his jacket pocket and produced a small device, which he handed to me. It consisted of an electrical gauge connected to a small wired plug.

"This is the Twattometer," he informed me. "It is a most ingenious device that allows you to gauge the precise level of twattiness emitted by any particular person or action."

I was overwhelmed by this courteous, practical gift, and offered him my hearty salutations for perfecting such a useful device.

"I am proud to say I own the patent on this, and expect to make millions. I should explain," continued he, "this device is for sale at Gavin's of Knightsbridge, price four shillings and sixpence.

"Gavin's of Knightsbridge?" I exclaimed with a gasp. "Then your success is assured."

"Well," smiled he, "I know you will find use for it."

"To business," called Holmes, having evidently decided that his personal foibles were being discussed at greater length than was comfortable. He flashed a brief smile that indicated his readiness to focus on the matter at hand. The Twattometer registered zero. I wondered if it was working.

Dr. Filbert became focused, his manner that of a man of science who is relating events that do not fit his experiences, even if they are entirely accurate.

"It is the most confounded thing," he began, his voice showing great bewilderment. "In my many years as a bonce engineer, I have never encountered one such matter, still less ten or twenty.

"My staff consist of psychiatric experts – loony attendants, if you will. Among them you will find London's finest nutter valets. All are committed to what they do, yet not one can offer me an explanation."

Holmes was clearly stirred by this revelation as it became clear we were indeed at the outset of a most singular case. It is true that my celebrated colleague has investigated professional matters that would weaken the stoutest, and indeed I have been overwhelmed on occasion.

"Ordinarily," the doctor continued, "the type of complaint varies but little. Our patients enjoy a stable, consistent environment that cannot ail them in the slightest."

He had brought a medical bag in with him, and from this he now produced a series of what looked like architectural plans. He spread these out over a table, weighting down each end.

"As may be seen from this diagram, beneath the House of Lords is a giant underground lunatic asylum. It used to be a huge wine cellar, and before that the world's largest underground ashtray.

"However, after the Crimea, it was decided to convert the area into a gigantic sanitorium. I have been privileged to serve as the custodian of this for no small amount of time, and in my thirty years' experience never have I encountered such bizarre events."

Here, all professional decorum having fallen from his demeanour, he leaned forward, his head in his hands. I had seen this happen many times before with Holmes' clients, but usually after he had started work.

"Just a moment, Dr. Filbert." Holmes chimed in. "I see you have consulted me before, in The Adventure Of The Recycled Joke." Pleased with his cleverness, Holmes preened and looked at us mere mortals with quiet content.

"He pointed that out on the first page," I muttered, rolling my eyes.

"Yes, my observational powers are quite remarkable," Holmes proudly congratulated himself as the Twattometer hummed into life.

"This is immaterial, gentlemen," our guest observed. "There is a matter of no little gravity at hand," he continued, ignoring Holmes rubbing his hands together and saying, "Goody!"

Here he produced some papers from his case. As we read them, it became clear where the problem lay.

"These are plans to allow the country to be run by apes," I was incredulous. "Why would anyone want to pass laws that allow the undead to hold high office?"

"I quite agree," our visitor looked mournfully perplexed. "It appears to be the work of a deranged subject, yet I cannot trace it."

"Can you think of anyone in your professional capacity who could have influenced this matter?" Holmes asked.

"Naturally, our roster includes a number of great senior politicians, who suffer a large amount of mental strain owing to the rigours of such positions. Extreme nervous fatigue could have informed these decisions. However, my enquiries were blocked at the highest level. There is worse to come, however."

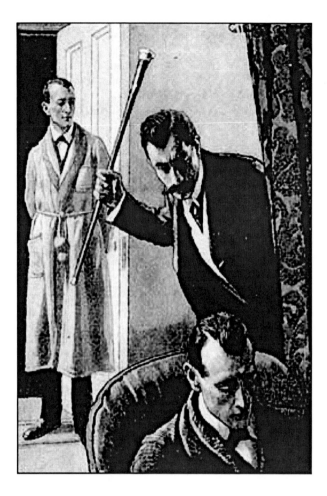

Holmes thought his stunt double was worth every penny.

"How so?" I asked, agape at his dread words.

"Experiments in the basement of the House of Lords have been discovered by senior men in government, who found them during a drunken raid on the wine cellars."

Holmes' expression tightened as he sensed the nub of the matter emerging.

"I would be obliged if you told me of every detail."

"Sadly, I can tell you little more. I do know that they found blood and paw prints, as though dangerous beasts were being housed. You must act quickly, for I know the clock is ticking. A great flurry of activity went on until the small hours. Something is imminent, make no mistake."

The doctor saw the time on the mantelpiece clock, whereupon his face fell. He muttered something about, "My God, the lateness of the hour ..." before he fled. This focused my celebrated colleague's mind still further.

The prospect of a highly unusual case brought a rush of rare speed from Holmes. Not even pausing to hail a cab, he raced round from our Baker Street flat to the Houses of Parliament, where the great and the good were considering matters of national importance.

I was out of breath when we arrived, for Holmes, when roused to one of his unusual bouts of energy, is a whirlwind. Not even pausing to taunt the beggar stood at the foot of Big Ben, he rushed up the steps to our nation's sanctum of democracy.

The great doors swung open at his approach. The notable Dr. Filbert had clearly been as good as his word, and telegraphed ahead of us. With one hand on the Twattometer in my pocket, I followed the great detective as he strode on, a purposeful air about him.

"Good day, I'm Mr. Sherlock Holmes. I believe you are expecting me."

"I wasn't, sir, owing to the fact that I am the tea lady. Would you like a cup?" replied the lady pleasantly.

"I do not require that particular beverage," Holmes replied with icy reserve.

"Ah. Well, the gin wagon will be along shortly, if you'd like a faceful of something a little stronger." She kindly passed me a bun, so I got something out of it.

I was chewing with relish as my esteemed colleague and I walked the corridors of power. Holmes made a point of keenly observing each passing lord as they trundled past, muttering importantly to themselves and, occasionally, each other.

We arrived at a great office. A clerk looked up at us from behind his desk.

"Hello sirs. How may I be of assistance?"

"My name is Sherlock Holmes."

"Be quiet, Watson," said my famous friend, swatting me across the head. "My cretin of an assistant here is joking, my good man. I am the famous detective, and our enquiries lead us here, the centre of our democracy."

I bridled at the blow, and made a mental note to smash his face in later, but here I could agree.

"True. So if there is to be any conflagration that threatens parliament, we'd like to be here to see it. Wait a moment," I corrected myself, "that came out wrong."

The clerk seemed puzzled.

"Who spoke to you?"

"Dr. Filbert, who I gather is a specialist here."

"Why yes, I of course know the gentleman. He is, however, away from his duties at the insistence of his superior, Lord O'Nion."

"You mean Onion?"

"No, his Grace is most particular that it is O'Nion. As it happens his Grace is without appointment at present. Please make your way through."

We moved to a waiting room with lavishly ornate fixtures. Shortly after this we were shown into an office where an elderly man sat behind a sizeable walnut desk.

"I am Mr. Sherlock Holmes, and I wish to arrest his Lordship for murder."

"Watson, stop doing that!" hissed Holmes, who moved to swat me again, only this time I waved a bunch of fives under his ruddy nose.

"I see," replied the elderly man. "Who is the deceased person?" he enquired, turning to a bulky journal.

"My colleague jests," Holmes informed him with an attempt at a spry smile. "I merely wish to confer over a matter of national importance."

"The personal assistant will arrange a time for your meeting that will not interfere with his Lordship's nap routine."

"That is most good of you," my salubrious friend purred. "Perhaps it would help if I pocketed some of these valuables while you attend to that?"

The old fellow behind the desk peered forward with some hesitation.

"I am not convinced that will be useful," murmured he. After turning over several pages, he convulsed slightly, eyes rolling backwards in his head so only the whites were visible. His mouth transformed into a ravenous gaping maw as his face was twisted into an inhuman vision, a walking incarnation of the foul.

A long and hideous gurgle rattled from his throat as a black snake like growth shot out of his mouth. As he bared his teeth we could see they were overformed and block-like, yellowed and menacing. A high pitched monkey screech emerged from him and he started grooming the post rack.

"I see this Victorian morality has driven another feller nuts," Holmes whispered.

"Tell me about it," I muttered. "I haven't had an indecent thought in months. Well, I'll leave you to it," and I left, leaving Holmes to make his appointment after the old buster finished convulsing. I visited the gentlemen's ablution chamber, for the sixteen cups of tea I had with breakfast needed expelling.

As I stood there splashing my boots, I noticed a great many flies around. There was the most unusual odour, not the dank urinal smell one might expect. Also, the floor was thick with treacle of a deep red colour, as though a great many jam puddings had been unrolled.

The ways of the rich aristocracy never cease to amaze me. Should I have been born into great wealth, I doubt I'd have wanted to walk about on desserts, but there we have it. They are richer than I, however, and so their ways are best.

Pausing to savour the majestic view of democracy in action, I peered into the debating chamber. The regular drone of issues being discussed was interrupted only by the steady hum of snoring and the occasional splutter of someone dying in their sleep. This was truly another fine day in Parliament.

I sat in the viewing gallery, overlooking the majesty of debate, taking in the finery of the scene. The grand robes sat well on many a distinguished shoulder, as the greatly advanced in years sat with senile precision on the issues of the day. This, I thought, is how weighty matters should be resolved – by ancient men far removed from the common folk, a majority of nearly one thousand ruling over our serene nation by dint of birth.

A steady humming of wings surprised my ears, as though a thousand giant bees were swooping from the heavens. From without the chamber a cry of terror was heard, and a great rattling shook the windows.

Splinters exploded through the air and the House of Lords was beset with winged monsters. They descended upon the Lords with a feral screeching, biting and gouging their way through the distinguished persons as though they were on an aristocrats only diet.

Great gouts of blood sprayed through the air and screaming tied with the sounds of torn limbs for the most horrific noise. It reminded me of last orders at *The Horse's Dong*, a particularly rough pub I frequented while impecunious. I will say, however, that patrons of that establishment rarely pulled someone's head apart to feast on the brainy goodness inside, which is a plus.

At first I sat stunned, a vision of hell unfolding before me. The creatures were everywhere, eviscerating and nibbling as they went. Certainly their table manners left a little something to be desired, as it is rare to eat with one's fingers in public, much less bite through the necks and skulls of persons to whom one has not been introduced.

I decided to move when a particularly nasty piece of violence covered the front of my sports jacket in goo. As that involved a spurt of over twenty feet, it was clear these brain chewers weren't kidding. Swine, I said to myself. Would any of these vicious beasts pay for the dry cleaning?

Amid the guts and devastation, my bulging eyes noticed a terrifying trend. Some of the dead – those less mutilated – were transforming into the same species that had killed them. From the newly changed, one of the more vicious creatures was still wearing his top hat, although his elongated flank had burst through his tailored coat. His snarling chimp face turned my stomach in shock.

I left the viewing gallery as soon as my senses were my own once more. Rushing to find Holmes, away from the deplorable slaughter, I questioned my own senses. What those creatures were I had no idea, for the experience was unprecedented in any

15

account. Nor had I any clue as to their involvement in the politics of the land, but I wondered if they were allowed to vote.

"Erm … if you want to scare me, I'm over here."

The corridors of power are many and varied. Soon the mayhem behind me could not even be heard. I searched for an official, but they all lay slumped in great pools of blood. Thinking this was very slapdash, I made a mental note to write a letter of complaint.

Soon enough I chanced across the clerk I had spoken to previously, still sat at his desk.

"I say, do you know where my friend and colleague Mr. Sherlock Holmes might be found?"

16

He trembled slightly as he turned to me, his composure somewhat rattled.

"Mr Holmes is still in Lord O'Nion's office. Please go straight through."

I did so, and saw Holmes crouched precariously on a grandfather clock. The doddering gentleman I had left him with was completely transformed, and was now one of the beasts I had seen before. He – or it – had not noticed my presence. For a moment I stood in the doorway, transfixed by the sight of this weird beast.

He had the basic build of a monkey, with a rich grey pelt. Wings sprouted from its back, and while these flapped feebly he could not raise himself move than an inch or two off the ground. From time to time his head twitched back and forth, and I saw it was still wearing gold pince-nez spectacles. A vile hissing noise emerged, and Holmes gibbered.

Quietly I slipped my revolver from my pocket and shot it in the head.

"Terribly sorry," I offered by way of commiseration. He slumped over, a growing red stain on the floor testament to my fatal shot.

The corpse was a vision of hell. This was the closest I had been to one of the creatures, and what perplexed me most was the purely black eyes and the stench of rotten meat. Its fangs were a coarse, fearsome sight, and the skin had become lined and grey.

"What happened?"

"He began some transformation just as you left," Holmes panted, now standing on the floor, his aspect still wild from the fright he had received. "It was a most fearsome and terrible spectacle to behold. Not five minutes after it began, he became a ferocious beast, some kind of winged monkey crazed for blood."

"Blimey," I observed. "In need of some medication, wouldn't you say?"

"This is unnatural indeed," observed he, his eyes narrowing. In moments he was a man of science and action once more. "We must assume these creatures have flooded the building. I see from your clear and decisive approach you have encountered more of these?"

"I have," I replied grimly. "The upper chamber was overrun by them, and I fear our country's leadership has been reduced to a simple matter of lunch."

"What a grave blow," Holmes murmured. "Our country's finest political minds dined upon to satisfy feral mutants. Now we must resolve the matter."

"Quite," I agreed, reloading my pistol.

The door opened. Holmes and I turned, a measure of dread in the movement. We were not, however, faced with some apparition from hell. Instead, a strikingly beautiful young woman stood looking at us, a cool deliberation in her manner. She came in and sat down.

"Can I help?" she asked, a smouldering sex appeal in her voice that had my feet pawing the ground. "I am Miss Ferguson, a humble assistant here."

"God, yes!" I replied, straightening my tie and putting on my best come-to-Watson smile.

Holmes stood over her, magnifying glass in hand, an expression of pure delight on his face. I shot him a warning glance as he copped an eyeful, suggesting he should take a calmer approach to this young lady, thus allowing me to apply my charms.

"Stick your tongue out," I suggested, cocking a jaunty eyebrow. Regrettably I have been a doctor too long and my seduction skills leave a little to be desired.

"Watson!" admonished Holmes. "That is no way to talk to a lady," said he, hanging a Deerstalker hat on his boner.

"We are in the middle of an intense piece of detective work," I offered. "Forgive our crass drooling, but it's been a long time since a woman has been in one of these stories."

She smiled and altered her posture, unleashing about 85 miles of legs.

"Great Scott," I mumbled. "I know the year is 1895, and the modern age is notoriously permissive, but good God, Holmes, I can see her knees!"

"Quiet," he hissed. "As you can see from the wretched, expired form on the floor, some bizarre species of creature is on the loose."

"This is true," I confirmed. "You should see the mess in the debating chamber."

"It's often the case during debates," she agreed. "Few of the Lords trouble to exercise proper bladder control, sadly, and often urinate in public. In fact, I think they enjoy it."

"I regret this is not quite what I meant. A great conflagration broke out, and I fear everyone in the forum was eaten. I fled the scene, I am not ashamed to admit, with the most ferocious belches echoing in my ears."

Miss Ferguson stood up. A ravishing vision of pure loveliness, she strode over to a cabinet and unlocked it. Taking out a book, she turned to Holmes.

"I feel this may contain the answers. Dr. Filbert was most concerned about a matter he would not discuss."

"How do you know he was concerned?"

"He would shudder and quake as he spoke of it, oftentimes trembling with fear and looking about him with the wild manner of a man possessed. That was something of a hint."

Holmes took the volume, leafing through it with concern etched on his features.

"It says here there is a diabolical experiment taking place underground, right here in Parliament. We must find the source of this evil in the laboratory."

"But Mr. Holmes," cried Miss Ferguson, showing a tender concern for my colleague that would have been better reserved for me. "Isn't that terribly dangerous?"

"I appreciate the concern, but danger is my business. Why, I remember during the infamous Felixstowe poisoning case, my life was despaired of."

"It still is," I added. "But he is right – do not fear for us. We merely do our duty. However," I continued as an afterthought, "should you wish to consider my efforts noble, selfless and utterly heroic, that is your right."

She sniffled modestly.

"I, too, have encountered terrible sights. I was returning from a most invigorating dump when I saw lamentable splatter."

"The slaughter is tragic," I agreed, angling for grief nookie.

"It grieves me to see my masters dead, so now I am ready to kick large amounts of monkey butt."

I was a little surprised by this last remark, but my ruminations were interrupted.

"Telegram for Mr. Holmes." We turned and saw a page, in full House of Lords servant regalia, standing smartly to attention as a monster sank its teeth into his free arm, which eventually dropped free. Like a good fellow, he stood there not making a fuss as the floor turned scarlet.

Holmes took the envelope, taking the trouble to peer closely at the smallest of details even as the page collapsed through lack of blood. I shot the creature that had, by this point, eaten most of him. I was kicking myself for not thinking of this earlier.

"It's from Dr. Filbert," Holmes informed me.

My immediate superiors have gone insane. They have unleashed a hellish plague of the living dead upon the capital, starting with Westminster and spreading to the suburbs as the situation dictates in re brains to eat. Regret you are fucked. As such, have gone to Eastbourne, where I will stay with my aunt until the matter blows over.

Toodle pip and no hard feelings

Your friend, Dr. F.

The chatline bill always horrified him.

"How dare he!" Holmes cried, vexed in a way I had never seen before.

"That's not so bad," I offered reasonably. "Why should he tell you before he goes on holiday?"

Holmes' reply was lost as the window shattered. A winged beast flew in, hovering near the ceiling for a moment or two, bearing its fangs and clawing the air. It screeched then settled, perched on the desk. Malevolence shone through its fierce black eyes, a hiss from the darkest night emanating from its maw. Bizarrely enough, the creature was impeccably dressed in a Saville Row suit.

The tremendous thunder of a shotgun blast rang in our ears as the creature's head burst. For a moment it stood, wings quivering and gore soaking its fine clothes. With a final jerk of its body the beast collapsed, never to rise again. I turned, seeing to my amazement Miss Ferguson standing there, a smoking shotgun in her grasp. She had adorned herself with a formidable variety of weapons.

"I must tell you what these creatures are," she informed us while reloading. "A dreadful experiment has been carried out here, one which transforms ordinary people into winged simians, dead but living."

"Why would anyone do that?" I asked, mystified.

"It was initially an administrative matter. Something to do with making meetings more efficient, but it took a dark turn. A man called Durbridge gained control. He is a lunatic who thinks he can control England with his undead freaks and their thirst for brains."

"So, they're flying zombie death monkeys?" asked Holmes, the most intelligent sentence he has uttered since the beginning of our friendship.

"That's the case. This one here," she indicated the headless mutant lying astride the desk, "will have transformed recently, for the condition is highly contagious. The sad thing is, by now they will be rampaging throughout the building."

A frenzied scratching at the door confirmed her statement. The snuffling noise without chilled my spine. Holmes reached into his pocket and produced a magnifying glass.

"Wrong call, old chap," I advised. "Try your revolver instead."

The door received several heavy blows. The three of us positioned ourselves in goodly fashion, firearms at the ready. Fragments of wooden frame burst in and a slavering mob of brutes crammed their hungry faces into the doorway. We opened fire at the swarm, dropping many of them with our well placed rounds.

The high pitched feeding snuffles of the creatures mixed with the shotgun books, and seemed to make the air blister. Our narrow view down the corridor was filled with shrieking monsters, the walls sprayed with gore. The fiends screeched more loudly at the sight of each of their fallen brethren, an array of grotesquely deformed beasts slumping into gouts of blood. In all my years in the army I never saw such a demented festival of brutality and savage death, not even during regimental parties.

Miss Ferguson and I continued firing as Holmes attempted to push the desk across the doorway. A particularly harsh bit of recoil pulled part of her dress away, revealing the kind of finery no medical book ever includes. My path of bullets chewed holes in the ceiling as I stood in rapt admiration.

"Thank God for that, some sex appeal." I yelled with enthusiasm, eyeing our new assistant with approval. "And a bit of gratuitous nudity. Nice one."

"It's purely essential to the plot," shouted Holmes above the pistol fire.

"Bullshit!" I yelled at him as another creature took a shot from my revolver.

It was lucky I had collected a parcel on my way out of our lodgings. It had rattled about in my coat for a while and, when I opened it, found that it rather handily contained a year's supply of bullets. Which, at the average rate of three bad guys a week, meant I was well stocked.

"Luckily I remembered to bring an unfeasibly large amount of ammunition for a Victorian detective story. Incidentally, I have a chainsaw on order, and one will be sent round the moment it's invented."

"A most thoughtful precaution, if I may say," Holmes complimented my wisdom. "I do not feel, however, that this aids us in our current predicament. We need to escape, find the root of this evil and somehow reverse it."

"A distraction is needed," I yelled. "Take your clothes off."

"Certainly," nodded Holmes, unbuttoning his shirt with alacrity.

"Not you!" I yelled, almost shooting him in irritation. "Her. Who the hell wants to be distracted by your hairy knees and third elbow?"

Before Holmes could answer, a fresh onslaught attempted to overrun our position. With not a word said between us we rushed down the corridor. Our footsteps clattered mightily, but could not compete with the scrabblings of the noxious hell beasts pursuing us for their dining pleasure.

I pride myself on the steel of my nerves, but the carnage behind me was too great for my courage. Skidding on a pool of blood, I pushed Miss Ferguson through an open office doorway. Holmes followed close upon our heels, slamming and locking the door as he did so. Momentarily, shards of wood flew from the door frame as the brutes clawed at it. The only sound to be heard was beasts outside a cage, howling to be let in.

"A shame we have no bananas," Holmes offered with a smile. I swore and made a mental note to kick him in the balls later. He sank into thought, becoming silent.

Miss Ferguson and I stood well back. Holmes' intellect was clearly working overtime, as he paced the floor in a neat line by the door. Such was the ferocity of venomous, blood crazed noise from the exterior that I wondered at his nerve. Still, the application of great intellect can allow for an isolation of concern, as was his demeanour now.

He turned to us with a focused yet quizzical expression.

"We need to understand these creatures," he spoke gravely. "Why is it they act the way they do, and what do they seek?"

"Brains!" I yelled. "Give them yours if you aren't using them." My loud words awoke a fresh scrabbling from outside, which spoiled Holmes' moment of cool indifference. With trembling hand, he held a finger to his lips.

"I have a suggestion. I have been listening to their movements, and when not engaged in pursuit, they are very slow. Their footsteps indicate a sporadic, shuffling type of motion, and one that leads me to believe we can thin their numbers greatly by means of selective attack."

Beckoning to where he stood, he gestured for me to get my gun ready and stand in wait. I did as directed, poised in readiness. From a silent count of three, he opened the door into the corridor, where the beasts had gathered. I pitched my aim at one, who was aimlessly moving back and forth, until he noticed my presence.

Suddenly fierce instincts shook the beast. It hissed at me, clawing the air with terrible menace as it closed in. I aimed carefully for its head and pulled the trigger. The heavy reverberation of the shot shook the corridor. A gouge of fur and blood hit the wall as the beast slumped into a heap of death.

I darted back into the room and Holmes slammed the door. Pleased with our success, we repeated it a number of times, accumulating a gratifying total. The zombies, with what remained of their minds evidently operating at a very basic level, largely ignored the onslaught. With their foes remaining hidden, they were apparently unaware that they were being attacked.

We spent a while doing this, Holmes operating the door while I leaned out and popped them one at a time. As we did so, Miss Ferguson stood by the window. She was closely observing events as they unfolded.

"This is appalling," cried she in sudden excitement. We paused in our efforts, staring at her. "There is a plague of them, a plague!"

Rushing over to where she stood, we both saw this was no lie. A veritable swarm of the bastards had gathered. They stretched as far as we could see, crowded in the streets, lumbering aimlessly with their strange insistent shuffling. A large number flew overhead, their speed a marked improvement on their ground work.

Burning buildings were dotted along the cityscape, the sign of who knew what further calumny. One zombie flew too close to one of the infernos and set himself ablaze. His flight screeched over our heads and straight into Big Ben. A titanic shattering crash made us flinch at the wretched beast's collision.

"Holy God, what can we do?" she cried.

"My dear, be calm," I assured her, in between clawing at the walls and screaming my lungs out. "There has to be a rational explanation for this, and my friend Sherlock is the one to find it," I counselled, my nose getting longer as I spoke. Holmes was busy studying the creatures' progress outside.

"How can he help us? I fear our situation, and this whole hideous mess, are beyond saving."

There was genuine despair in her manner, which made me feel desperately protective. This young woman was faced with a dire, inexplicable peril. I resolved to set her mind at rest as far as I could.

"We are in good hands, for Holmes is the best at what he does."

"The best?"

"Beyond question," I lied. "The man is a genius."

She wrinkled her face in reproachful disbelief.

"There are two kinds of genius. People like Michelangelo, and the man in the pub who can play Spice Girls songs on the accordion."

"Quite," I murmured in surprise, wondering what she was referring to. I could only surmise that she was very ahead of her time.

"What will Holmes do?" she pressed, the urgency in her eyes mixed with sardonic amusement, as my over celebrated colleague stood at the window and experimented, a feather in each hand. I wondered where he got them.

"Wait. I can't hear anything from outside." Miss Ferguson beckoned us over. Holmes put down his feathers and crept over to the door. Opening it slightly, we could see the creatures had indeed left.

We inched our way along the corridor, every moment tense enough to quicken our already drawn nerves. For several anxious minutes the three of us sought an exit, edging along as silently as we could. From around the corner the loping, scrabbling of paws could be heard. In an instant, Holmes and I stood paralysed.

Turning to a closed door, Miss Ferguson fired at the lock and we burst in, breathless. We both stood with our backs pressed firmly against the wall to deal with any intruders.

We had blundered into some type of appointment, evidently a form of analysis. Sat in a chair was an earnest looking therapist, leaning forward and taking notes. A man was lying on a couch. One of the zombies, crouched behind him, was quietly eating his brains with little slurping noises and using an egg spoon.

I gathered this had been someone of refinement before his grotesque turning.

The doctor had his eyes fixed on his notebook, and had not noticed the creature. He was paying rapt attention to the fellow on the couch, who was talking about his ailments.

"The thing is, I've been suffering from these terrible headaches."

"I see," he observed steadily. "And how long has this been bothering you?"

"Well, since you ask, it's ever since this weird beastie has been chewing through my cranium."

The therapist peered up and made an 'ah, yes' noise.

"Even so, it could be due to overwork," offered the quack.

"Right you are," confirmed the patient, surprisingly cheerful for a man who was having his head eaten. "What about these headaches?"

"Ah, well, I'd avoid having strange creatures eat your brains," advised the doctor. Stout fellow. In his position, I'd have said much the same.

Noticing an adjourning side door, we crept out. Leaving the matter alone without dealing with it was not ideal, but we dared not risk the noise. The next corridor was mercifully deserted and we hastened along.

Shortly before we reached its end, a well dressed and agitated man burst out of a side door. We were all stunned with shock, until it became apparent this gentlemen, seventy if he was a day, started to speak.

"Mr. Holmes! I have information for you, sir."

He was about to speak further when a fiend sprang from behind, landing on him. With great relish it began chewing through his skull. Holmes screeched in terror. I aimed a volley of shots at the beast, but it fled.

"It is that arch fiend Durbridge!" cried the man in his dying throes.

"What's a throe?" he gargled, then lay back, completely still.

"I assume he's dead?" Holmes enquired.

"He isn't moving, so let's take that as read," I confirmed. "Plus, most of his brains have been eaten." The more I thought about it, the harder it was to escape. "Yes, he's dead."

"Thank God one of us studied medicine," Holmes observed with a grimace. "Otherwise I'd have expected him to spring into life singing and dancing. However, at least we now have some information on which to build."

"I'll check the records library, too see what can be found there. You must check the basement, find where Dr. Filbert was working and check for clues."

"Right," I confirmed. "Come with me," I said to Miss Ferguson, doing my best heroic man of action walk.

"This way, quickly." She grabbed my wrist in a steel grip. "We must go through the catacombs." Her urgency was compelling. I saw Holmes disappear into the library as Miss Ferguson unlocked a door. She beckoned me to follow her.

We made our way down a narrow stone staircase, each step echoing into the dark. Despite being well armed, I shuddered internally as we descended into the near black basement. Intense thin columns of light shocked their bright way through the gloom, bringing the puddles of dank water into brilliant life in the reflections.

As we walked along, the grids at the base of the walls rattled, shaken by creatures of immense strength. Hisses of monumental anger seeped along the corridor. It was an eerie sensation, finding ourselves surrounded by the anger of beasts we could not see.

"This must have been where the creatures were kept until the time was right," Miss Ferguson told me. "It makes sense, from what I've seen. Hopefully they're all confined."

An enraged face burst from the empty shadows. Its bestial features were tautened by bloodlust it could barely contain. It howled with terrible rage, shocks of jagged white teeth bared and snapping.

The zombie hissed at Miss Ferguson, it's foul jaws raging at her as its dark eyes glared into hers. For a terrible moment she was transfixed, the beast's face mere inches from her own. It was so close that I dared not shoot. With a blink the spell was broken, and she regained her senses, swung up the shotgun and blasted the contents of its head on the ceiling.

"There'll be more," she commented. "I can hear them. Let's set a trap."

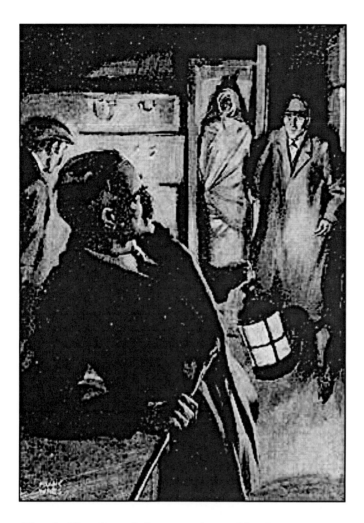

"Look, I've found the extra large hip flask!"

Spraying perfume as a lure, she left a trail leading into the dank grotto around an inlet pipe. We stood poised for a time, both silent during the wait. Twin metallic reflections shone along the deadly muzzle of her shotgun.

Soon we heard the snuffle of a creature, the low scraping of its movement preparing us. Miss Ferguson's face was tense. As she moved with silent efficiency the light darted electrically along the barrels in two lines of certain death. The retort within the tightly enclosed space was deafening, and appeared to rattle the tiles.

"That was close," I whispered, looking at the grisly remains only a few feet of us.

"That's not all. Someone was expecting us," she commented grimly, gesturing upwards.

I looked up to see blades poised by the ceiling. Their edges held an evil glint, the promise of swift evisceration. The grim sheen of honed metal was an appalling contrast to the stone.

"We should leave," I decided. "There's nothing here but death and puddles. One wrong move and we'll be trapped."

We retraced our steps to the main corridor. It was dark. The illustrious trappings of red and gold trim were now rendered sinister by the few lights that flickered intermittently on. After such confinement and threat, I found my mood lightening considerably as we put distance between ourselves and the catacombs.

"I don't see why a monogamous relationship can't be sleazy," I was saying, reasonably, when Miss Ferguson silenced me.

"Ssh! Someone's coming."

A smartly dressed man made his way toward us, his step faltering with nerves. From the feeble noise he made in attracting our attention, I would hazard that he was well stricken in years.

It was then we saw the transformation process of the fallen at close quarters. Firstly, his back arched. He began turning circles on the ground as his legs propelled him round. His jaws champed in near frenzy, saliva pouring from his lips. Thick downy hair spouted at every juncture along his skin as his limbs elongated.

A wrenching agony pulled his face taut, the jaw straining to its furthest degree. Initially I was too stunned to move, but upon recovery I made my way over. Transforming from man to beast in a few seconds appalled me, and I almost felt sorry for him as I aimed my gun.

As the shot rang out, Holmes poked his head from a nearby doorway.

"All done?"

"I think we need to leave. The place is overrun."

"True. The library is full of human remains, and none of them are filed correctly."

Galvanised by this thrilling development, we rushed out of the building. Miss Ferguson took the lead, covering the way with a rifle. I moved quickly along, but Holmes lagged behind.

"You can have more weapons later."

"We must find the source of this problem," he announced grandly, as we the tattered trio of survivors limped our way onwards.

"That should be easy," I snapped with some heat. "It's a lot of winged undead brain ingesting monkey bastards who want to banquet on our heads. There," I stopped still, ticking points off on my fingers. "I believe I've covered everything."

Holmes and I stared at each other for a moment, the wordless seething between us fraying many years' friendship and respect. Such anger between two men of iron will could not but end badly, perhaps even tragically.

My fingers twitched toward the butt of my revolver, and Holmes' hand slowly eased its way towards the pistol tucked into his belt.

"That's enough of that." Miss Ferguson's voice was firm and clear, her manner that of one who would stand no nonsense. The mechanical sound of shells being pushed into a rifle breech cooled our violence.

"Honestly, you men! Bring on a lot of flying chimps and you go all to pieces."

She strode toward without the smallest glance back. Her haughty resolve stirred me deeply, although I felt quite the fool. Holmes himself appeared far from his aloof, masterful self.

"Are you two coming, then?" she called back after reaching the end of the street. Stood majestic and alone, her face framed against the sky, she looked magnificent with her rifle slumped nonchalantly over her shoulder.

We made our way toward her, resolving to leave the matter alone, at least until we were away from the disapproving eyes of our trigger happy friend. Overhead, the sky darkened. Holmes looked at his watch, puckering in consternation.

"Most unusual for a little past noon," he observed. As he spoke, a severed arm fell at his feet. We both stared at it for an uncomprehending moment, before looking up into the zombie filled sky.

"Run!" called Miss Ferguson, her voice cracking with panic. She fired into the vast flock of flying undead. A splash of blood danced briefly in the air as we took to our heels. While we ran, the shadows of intensely flapping beasts raced us along the ground. A chorus of bestial grunts echoed above our heads as more than once I felt the scratch of a talon along my back.

"Mr. Dickens is here to improve the writing, sir."

A flurry of shots rang out as Miss Ferguson blasted away at the terrific peril swooping overhead. It was only when we reached her at the end of the street that we looked back to gauge the seething mass behind us. A fearsome sight it was, too. Their drooling jaws snapped for our flesh. It seemed that our doom was at hand when something caught my attention.

"Quick, in here," I shouted, booting down the door of a nearby pub. We piled in, aghast and breathless from the peril left behind. Grabbing tables and chairs, we barricaded the door with incredible speed.

"By the Queen's best hat, that was good thinking, Watson." We were all shaken, exhausted by our terrible ordeal. I could only nod my thanks to Holmes.

"You don't have to block the door to have a quiet pint," announced a voice behind us. We turned in some surprise and found ourselves facing a dour looking bartender. His disapproval was clearly matched by the numerous patrons. Evidently their view was that we didn't belong.

"Have you seen what's out there?" Holmes asked as we rearranged our composure and reloaded. Miss Ferguson then turned to the pub's clientele.

"There's a scourge outside that is unlike anything you've ever seen," she told them, her voice stricken with a pleading note, imploring them to believe her.

"Really?" piped up one chirpy fellow, who clearly wasn't too bright. "What's that then?" he asked, and before anyone could stop him he stuck his head out of the window to have a look.

A terrible noise of rapid chewing could be heard, and the man's body writhed hideously. Blood geysered all over the windows, as soon enough his headless corpse slumped to the floor.

"That's some fierce rain," observed one of the locals.

"Aye. Best take an umbrella," said another, before calling for another beer.

The three of us exchanged glances.

"I assure you, with all earnestness, that the most dire, unimaginable peril lies just beyond those doors," Holmes intoned gravely.

Despite the decapitated form dripping all over the floor, they still mocked.

"Bollocks, it's only a bit of rain," scoffed one. "I'll prove it," he said brightly, putting on a light mac and stepping outside before anyone could stop him.

His screams lasted but a moment. Blood seeped under the door, which I had been careful to rebarricade. This time there was a reaction, and a fierce one at that.

"The bastards!" cried one voice in outrage.

"Revenge!" chimed up another patron, draining his beer at a gulp and throwing the glass to the wall. "Kill them!"

A bloodthirsty roar swept over the boozer. These liquored up souls were aflame for vengeance. It was most gratifying, for we had gone from just three hunted survivors to being part of an angry mob thirsty for violence. The odds had shifted in our favour.

Briefly, we explained the situation. They listened with some astonishment.

"Right. Tool up then," called the barman. An assortment of makeshift weapons were assembled. Bottles were smashed and legs pulled off tables, while a number of them produced knives. In no time the hostelry had gone from being a restful boozer to a budding war zone.

"Here's how it goes down," instructed the bartender, a natural leader in this situation. "There'll be three waves of attack. First, the snooker lads. You go out first, with any bits of cutlery you can find taped to the end of the cues.

"You'll break a hole in the ranks. Second up, the darts players. You can take some of them out from a distance. Remember, go for the head. Eyes and ears count as double points.

"That should give us some space. The rest of us will pile out and stab, gouge, slash, disembowel, decapitate, dismember and dispatch every last brain chewing bastard we can find.

"Win or lose, live or die, all your tabs are wiped clean. Who's with me?"

There was an impressive clamour of approval. The blood of these fine people clearly boiled for revenge, and a spirit of viciousness pervaded the air.

No drums rolled as the first wave readied for the off, nor could any ravens be heard in morbid song above. I should imagine they'd all been eaten, for one thing. Only a still air of anticipation was with us.

"Easy does it."

Two men stood either side of the doors, easing the bolt back in readiness. The masterful bartender stayed them with a gesture.

"This is it." I cocked my revolver. "Now." The doors were flung open.

If I were waiting for hell on earth to unleash itself, I was to be disappointed. There was a quick adrenaline rush as the first wave rushed out, fully braced to stab their makeshift weapons into the hoard of winged demons that weren't there.

The bartender strode forward to assess the situation. As our self appointed leader, he clearly considered it his role to be first out and into the open. Given the appalling carnage we'd seen these creatures perpetrate, I for one was not going to stop him.

"There's not a sign of them," he confirmed. "Not a whisper. Either we scared them off, or they just left anyway. Ah well, drinks on the house."

A rush of goodwill greeted this statement, as all clamoured for the bar. Order was restored and regularity came with it. Pints were ordered and knocked back as bar room games resumed. I marvelled at how these worthy types could be prepared to risk life and limb one moment, and be content with their ale the next. It was a most happy occurrence that we found this place, I decided.

Some time later we were ensconced at a table, discussing the hideous events over a brandy. The exhaustion of the day had taken its toll, and Miss Ferguson had dozed off. I had settled into a reverie, sat staring at my glass. Previously lost in thought, my celebrated colleague began talking.

"This lull in violence has allowed me to study these beasts," Holmes informed me.

"Excellent," I was cheered by this news. "Have you spotted a weakness?"

"Yes. They don't like having their heads cut off. Otherwise, no. These bizarre creatures are most peculiar. When airborne they are extremely agile, as their powerful wings afford them considerable propulsion. However, as soon as they land on terra firma, their movement is limited to that of a walking ape corpse, a zombie chimp, if you will."

I was intrigued.

"Are you suggesting we can find these brutes and pacify them with tea parties?"

"Sadly, no. It appears their appetites are solely for blood, gizzards and guts, but most specifically brain proteins."

"Good God!" I was stunned and not a little disgusted by this horrific data. "How long have you spent observing them?"

"Well, I've been looking at this one for about five minutes now."

I looked up to see Holmes peering at a creature through his magnifying glass. It appeared to be mollified by the reflections. As soon as I made eye contact it snarled hideously, a terrifying menace suddenly leaping into its manner.

It roared at Holmes, blaming him for the situation, and leapt at him. Holmes ducked as the creature sailed over the table, landing at the feet of some snooker players. With a fierce growl it pounced on one of the unlucky fellows. An arm flew through the air.

A massive cry of shock echoed round the room, followed by a vicious stampede of retribution. The beast was mauled, stabbed and kicked to oblivion in a fierce blizzard of pub violence. What remained of the beast was pasted to the wall in a grisly display of winged ape modern art.

There was a whoop of delight from the regulars. It appeared that our enemy had struck, caused some mild carnage and then been trounced. Victory was ours, with a sense of joy prevailing.

The exhilaration of that moment was terrific, although sadly fleeting. A slow, uncomfortable realisation passed. While we, the humans, were huddled inside, our foe had surrounded us.

We were sheep in a pen, with the wolves gathered outside. At every window, outraged and poised, the glowering undead faces watched. What they waited for, I knew not.

For the briefest of moments Holmes became overwhelmed at the dire extent of our situation.

"Say something, Watson."

"Shit."

He gulped for a moment.

"I agree."

Somehow, the zombies had understood our plan. They had disappeared, doubled back and were waiting outside to devour us. This meant that Sherlock Holmes, one of the cleverest men in the country, had been outwitted by a gang of deceased chimps. It was not a thought that promoted optimism.

We had little time for panic, although I managed to cram quite a lot of it into the few seconds we did have. I heard no signal, but at some sign a great scrabbling began all around us. The drinkers assembled themselves as best they could, fuddled by booze and a false sense of security.

The bartender rallied our spirits as best he could.

"Lads... lads! We can win this. They may have us cornered, but what are they, after all? Undead monkeys? Get the better of us? I've never heard anything so ..."

He never finished his rousing speech. One of the biggest, most savage apes sprang into the room and grabbed him. For one horrific second his ragged form sprayed the room red, turning the snug barroom into an abattoir. The man was shaken for several terrible moments, his tattered remains then flung aside by the beast.

It raged into the thick of the pub clientele, a killing machine snuffing out lives with the determination of a tidal wave. We ducked down and fired at the creature, our bullets ploughing into it but scarcely slowing it down.

Through the midsts of this hideous carnage, I looked to the windows. Still the eager faces of the deceased monkeys looked in. It became apparent that they regarded him as a champion, some sort of wonder chimp, to make a great impact for them.

I could understand their confidence, for the creature was a most terrible spectacle to behold. Unlike the regular specimens of this menace, he was not interested in eating brains, just pulling people limb from limb, which he did with gusto.

It was raining arms and legs for a while. We attacked him as best with could with bullets, knives, darts, beer glasses and anything else that came to hand. He seemed unstoppable. Shot after shot burrowed into his vast flank, riddling his torso with holes.

Braying with tortured beast lungs, the creature lashed out time and again. The fearful effect of his actions dripped all over the room, nor was it possible to take a step without leaving a footprint of gore. Battling against his vast strength was a hideous experience, truly unsettling as the creature absorbed shockwave after shockwave of horrendous violence without succumbing.

The great battle looked set to continue for a while, as apparently we had caused little damage. For all the telling injuries he'd suffered, we may as well have been tickling the brute. Something was needed to turn the tide, for we were running out of people to be mauled to pieces.

I was aiming at the ugly brute's head, ready to put a third or fourth shot into his astonishingly thick skull. His resilience to our onslaught was horrendous. Sooner than squeeze off another ineffectual round, by some inspiration I looked above. An old chandelier was positioned perfectly above the beast's head. I drew my breath in, took careful aim for its cable and scored a bullseye.

The ornate light fixture crashed down solidly onto the doomed monster's head, causing it to buckle to the floor. It began hissing wildly, a sign that its fierce terror was over.

It was finished with a neat slice across the neck, administered with fine panache by Holmes. Miss Ferguson knocked its head off by bludgeoning it with a fierce swipe of her rifle.

A bizarre unified cry of dismay echoed from outside as the zombies realised their champion had fallen. The frenzied hum of a hundred winged backs rose through the air. The sound was like a swarm of angry bees, only bees that were also gorillas. I wondered if they made honey. A battle anthem of unusually aggressive grunts could be heard.

We had no time to tend the dead and dying, not that there would be much point tending the dead. Our spirit of fierce combat had no time to abate, as the onslaught was immediate and intense.

A colossal screech of vengeance met our ears. Their attack was merciless. It was a veritable storm of flying teeth, snapping and chewing as they razed their way through the room. For the second time within the hour the poor patrons suffered a murderous attack from unnatural creatures.

Anybody who claims that the average English drinker isn't a man of steel and dedication is talking nonsense. These brave fellows waded into the enemy with their all. I have never seen glasses being smashed into the faces of blood crazed members of the undead before, but it made a hell of an impression.

The battle was fierce and raged with a violence too intense for the mind to comprehend. My recollection of it is as of a dream, a series of half-remembered episodes that knit together shambolically. A shriek of pain here, a flying head there. The carnage was intense while the battle raged, but with fortitude, keen marksmanship and a goodly supply of luck, we prevailed. The creatures fled, leaving many of their number behind, in pieces.

The attack had taken a horrific toll. The corpses did not lie in heaps, as for the most part their mutilation was too great too allow this. I did think of sweeping all the feet into one corner, the arms into another and so forth, but where would I stop? Making a big pile of ears on a table seemed a little morbid. Momentarily too stunned to move, I drank the scene in silently.

The epic battle was finished. Bodies lay strewn around like death was going out of fashion. Holmes staggered forward, his Deerstalker tattered from where an attempt was made to dine on his grey matter.

An occasional moan could be heard from the wounded on the ground, whose suffering was as mighty as their cause was just. Although battered and shaken from the vicious fray we had survived, Holmes was concerned for the wounded.

"Watson, get these men aid."

"Certainly. Ale or lager?"

"This is no time to fool around. Get the brandy, also ice and the posh glasses. If they're going to die on the battlefield, they may as well do so in style."

"I'll bring cigars, too. But what if they turn?"

Holmes' jaw set.

"We'll just have to deal with them. A grisly task, to be sure. Perhaps you can ask Miss Ferguson to assist? It strikes me as an odd duty to ask of a woman, but she has proven herself more than capable."

As I gazed around a sombre sight met my eyes.

"I agree, but I'm afraid she won't be able to help. She's dead."

Holmes looked stricken, his mouth opening and closing silently several times. At last he found his voice.

"Are you sure?"

"Well, if that's her head over here," I pointed left, "and that's her body there," I pointed right, "then I would say I'm sure."

My celebrated colleague's demeanour sagged.

"That's a blow. She was going to shag me when all this was finished."

I could appreciate that in moments of high drama men are wont to talk bollocks, but this terrible presumption could not pass.

"You're deluded, old friend. It was me she had the hots for. She told me as much, while bellowing at me for being an anus on legs."

Holmes' expression lapsed into a supercilious veneer. Clearly my words had hit home, for he became aloof, evidently recognising how accurate I was.

"I fear you may be mistaken," he weaselled quietly, then coughed sharply.

I may have looked up guiltily, as I noticed he was looking over my shoulder and reading the notes I was taking, in preparation for my memoirs.

"I take exception to that," he snapped, eyes ablaze. "Besides, what the hell is a 'supercilious veneer,' you turd?"

"Holmes, Holmes," I pacified him. "We are in the middle of a great adventure, stricken with threats and violence. In the middle of this, the death of a young woman has come between us, solely because you refuse to accept the overwhelming attraction she had for me. You are deluded."

There was a long pause.

"Quite," said Holmes slowly. "I think not. However," once more he become his aloof, precise self, "it would be unfortunate if we were to bicker over the supposed fancies of a dead woman. It is but a trifling affair."

At that moment, I couldn't have been more offended if Holmes had told me Miss Ferguson was a thief, her personal hygiene was lacking and that she was ground breakingly ugly with it. I resolved to smash his stupid face in the minute the mystery was over.

A stricken patron coughed. He was a hideous mess, lying mauled amid the gore. His face was pale, near enough the only sight that wasn't grizzled red. He beckoned me close with trembling fingers. When I got close enough, he whispered to me.

"Did some terrible lesion of the mind create this heinous manifestation of hell on earth? Are we being punished for our sins by the divine forsaking us for the ungodly?"

"Crikey, those are good questions," I agreed, but before I could answer fully, his eyes rolled upwards and life left his body. I watched him for a few mournful seconds before readying my revolver, and doing what must be done.

"There's a lot of dead bodies here," I observed. "We must decapitate each one, lest they turn into creatures and eat our brains."

Holmes looked about him with some disdain.

"Nah. Let's blow the place up."

"Fair enough," I agreed. It was both practical and efficient.

Utilizing some paraffin from the cellar we made short work of incinerating the remains. As we left flames were licking the outside of the bar. The windows burst from the heat and roof sizzled above the inferno.

"It seems democracy in this country is being besieged by a new, sinister species of ape," Holmes stated as we walked away from the burning building.

"So that's why the creatures all left the pub at the same time?"

"That's right. The division bell sounded to signal a vote, so they left. Now we now must follow them, return to the scene of the outbreak, and stop it."

The streets of London had undergone a marked change since our fight. All the buildings seemed far more dank and antiquated than I remembered, possibly due to the absence of thronging people. With no bustle and cheer in the streets the place was completely changed. The few people we saw out looked haggard and drawn, as though some terrible plague was breathing down their necks.

As we walked towards Westminster and the Houses of Parliament, it became clear that some terrible curtain had been drawn over the capital. The streets had grotesque smears of blood on them at frequent intervals. Many of the shop fronts were tattered, the remains of their owners and customers inside, chewed and mutilated beyond recognition.

Despite this, there were still pockets of almost fierce good cheer. We walked down one road that looked as though a street party were in progress. People mingled with creatures, drinking beer and apparently swapping witty anecdotes. Holmes and I marvelled at the bizarre spectacle and wondered at its cause, which became apparent when we got nearer.

A group of cheering spectators were gathered in a ring, greatly exhilarated by a competition. One gnarled costermonger used his giant fists to stun the brutes in a series of one on one bare knuckle bouts. It was a most unusual sight, as the monkeys were subdued, evidently absorbed in watching several of their own kind having their teeth knocked out by one muscular fellow.

"Good show," called out Holmes in approval, whereupon the brutes' expressions changed. Rapt wonderment turned to vicious consternation, at which point they abruptly slaughtered everyone. My celebrated colleague watched in dismay as the exuberant crowd were mauled to shreds and eaten.

"Don't mention that in the book," Holmes implored, somewhat shamefaced.

"Of course not," I assured him. It's good to have friends.

We left the street somewhat awkwardly, continuing apace without distraction. When we neared our destination, I noticed the statue of Oliver Cromwell outside Parliament had been well and truly crapped on, so buried was his likeness in monkey shit. We had no time to pause for political commentary, so we left the likeness as it was.

Outside the House of Lords, uniformed soldiers guarded the door, as they had before the outbreak. Had they somehow not been aware of recent events, I wondered?

It does you credit to still be at your post," Holmes informed them. "Have any more strange events occurred?"

"You mean, since the gigantic outbreak of savage flying beasts with an insatiable craving for human flesh?" asked one of the soldiers, scratching his head thoughtfully. "Not that I can think of. Here, Brian," he called to his colleague. "Anything unusual been going on?"

"What, outside a massive undead chimp reanimation virus breaking out?" he paused. "Well, the tea tasted unusual this morning." Holmes cocked an eyebrow and scribbled this down.

"That may be significant. We shall continue our enquiries inside. I wish you great luck with guarding the door."

"Don't worry," Brian assured us. "If thousands of ravenous monsters turn up, charging over the bridge, we'll deal with them."

Leaving the two of them stood confidently at their post, we proceeded through the gigantic ornate doors. Inside was an eerie quiet. There were thousands of claw marks on the walls, the fine ornate carpets had been chewed to pieces and there was ape shit everywhere.

"Things have changed," murmured Holmes.

"It is a little different."

"We must proceed carefully."

Slowly we walked down the main corridor, moving with great caution. The echoes of our footsteps rang ominously down the long expanse. A chill ran down my spine, into my shorts, across my knees and into my socks, where it hid. It was, indeed, a moment of massive apprehension.

At the side was a door marked "Legal Department." We opened the door and saw within dozens of chewed, dismembered corpses.

"Well, at least they've eaten all the lawyers," I observed with a grim sense of satisfaction.

"True, Watson," agreed Holmes. "It's an ill wind that blows no good. But we cannot sit here counting our blessings. Those creatures will return to make a light lunch of our grey matter before long. We must see what is at the root of this, and destroy it."

"I agree."

We spent some tense minutes rooting through papers. Both of us started with the drawers headed 'Secrets.' I had no idea the government would lack subtlety so badly. We rummaged through the files for a while when I made a striking discovery.

"Great Scott," I exclaimed with fervour. "Did you know Shakespeare used to host a game show called *Yank My Pizzle* during the intervals of his plays?"

Holmes sat thoughtfully for a moment, pretending his mind was on higher things.

"Watson, if I told you that the entire British government was at stake, would you despair?"

"Of course not," I replied cheerfully. "Look at them."

We found no clues, and so resumed our way down the long, newly sinister corridor of power. It appeared to take an eon to walk perhaps three hundred feet. A large pair of forbidding black doors awaited us at the end. Taking a deep breath, we opened them. We were prepared for anything, fearing the worst and ready to die.

The debating chamber had undergone a horrific transformation. The gilded benches on which members sat were smashed, broken and trampled to the ground. The lavish carpets beneath our feet were soaked with blood. We left gruesome scarlet footprints as we walked.

"Good evening, gentlemen."

The voice was deep and somewhat hollow, as though strands of its humanity had been removed. Amid the sights of carnage and devastation we hadn't noticed him. The man addressing us was an odd looking fellow. His head was largely bald, with thriving tufts of white hair curled around the edges. His eyebrows were boldly black, circling at their either end into a hook.

"Ah, Mr Holmes. So good of you to drop by. I suppose you identified me some time ago?"

"I've no idea. Who the hell are you?" Holmes swotted at me with his pistol.

"Ignore him. I'm Holmes. I keep telling him about that."

The man with the sinister bonce sent a piercing look my colleague's way,

"I've been waiting a long time for this, Mr Holmes," intoned he with evil relish. "Pull my finger."

The villain ran off with the plot.

Holmes ignored the proffered digit. Looking momentarily outraged, our host with the eccentric hair continued.

"I see you have an aloof approach, Mr Holmes. Let me assure you I am no common criminal. My name is Miles Durbridge. I believe you've met my creatures. Their existence is my discovery, and the world's terror."

"You're mad."

"They called Napoleon mad. They called Nero mad. They called Caligula mad."

"They were mad."

His face crumpled in rage for a moment, then settled into calm. He beckoned us to the windows and pointed at the view. His smile was a gloating display of malice.

"Look out at the change I have created."

The damage to London was horrific. We had not been far into the capital since the matter had started, and had no idea of how far the carnage had been spread. Stood in the debating chamber of the House of Lords, we were now able to see. From our high vantage point, and the view it commanded, we were able to appreciate the full horror of the destruction he had wrought.

For a moment, Holmes was sunk. His aloof, calculating machine mind was grasping to understand the situation.

"So you see, the world is indeed changing."

Holmes turned away from the window for a moment. The cog wheels of his intellect were turning in vain, helpless as Durbridge pointed out a quiet row of composed simian zombies, all sat earnestly engaged upon reading the minutes from a committee meeting.

With the scattered limbs, brain residue and carnage, it was the debating chamber of hell's own arse. 'Dissenters will be eaten' was written in blood on the walls.

"Isn't there a problem with same species dining?" asked Holmes. Miles Durbridge paused.

"There are outbreaks of rabidly unpredictable behaviour, but who's going to notice?"

"A good point," Holmes replied grimly. "And the people haven't revolted?"

Durbridge mused for a moment.

"A thorny question," he conceded. "There have been a few unhappy citizens, but they aren't around to follow up their complaints. I have been posting my minions to them, and as soon as they open their mail are devoured without mercy."

"Why bother mailing them?" I had to ask.

"Much easier than expecting them to follow directions," he explained patiently, waving a hand dismissively toward his row of zombie apes, all sat doing paperwork of some legal nature or another.

"This will be the beginning of a new world. A world run by undead monkeys who can fly, and all because I was bullied as a child." He turned to us apologetically. "I agree, it's not the best reason, but there you go."

Holmes began playing for time. It is often wise to engage these dominance aspiring sociopaths in conversation about their fiendish schemes, the better to lure them off balance.

"All this mayhem, the disruption of species, and playing God. How did you make this happen?"

"By will. I set this entire chain of events in motion through sheer focus. I sat and I thought, exerting every corner of my mind. As I brought forth every last segment of effort I possibly could, a whole new vista of possibilities was opened up. For a while I laboured in vain. It was a lot like constipation.

"Around this time, I was hired at the House of Lords, where I first met Dr. Filbert. With my qualifications, it did not take long before   I was put in charge of his medical storage facility in the catacombs. It was a prime opportunity to continue my research. Also, I discovered a chamber full of weird gizmos and bizarre shit in the basement that came in handy."

"You laboured to create these horrors here, under the very nose of Parliament and British democracy?"

"I did indeed. Nobody bothered me, for there were few enquiries into what went on. Day after day issues of vast importance were debated by those whose influence was a birthright. Not a vote was cast. In the meantime, I conducted a variety of unnatural experiments. Little by little, my efforts were rewarded. Then came a breakthrough, from an unexpected source. I've had to dispense with him. But after that, the effects were momentous."

"Now you have told me how you developed your work. What else?"

"Dr Filbert became suspicious, so he had to go."

"Ah. So you've killed him then?"

Durbridge looked surprised.

"No. He had to go, on holiday to his aunt's house in Eastbourne."

The Man With The Evil Bonce, as I now thought of him, looked at us with relish.

"I suppose you're wondering how you're going to die?"

My colleague looked thoughtful for a moment.

"Well, I always thought I'd probably keel over after a hearty lunch, aged about eighty."

"I think he means more quickly than that."

Durbridge let slip another evil chuckle.

"I experimented on my political lords and masters. Their minds went, at least, those that hadn't already gone. Then they become zombies, although that passed without comment. In fact, they fitted in nicely.

"It became an obsession. Something relentless and inexorable drove me. I considered it my meaning in life. Working where I did only encouraged me. I, too, yearned to talk bollocks and be taken seriously. I realised my experiments could make this happen. I recharged my ambition, injected it with a healthy dose of not giving two hoots for the consequences and continued."

"I doubt you will succeed."

"If that's the case, Mr. Holmes, then I will cancel my subscription to Evil Genius magazine, which intends to feature me on the cover of the next issue."

Our foe, creator of a plague of hell, glowered at us with determined malice. He pointed to where we stood and gestured us to another area. Holmes moved along, motioning for me to do the same.

"I would like to draw your attention to the trapdoor." I kicked Holmes. "Beneath are special tanks I had constructed, containing the much feared bollock fish, so named for their method of attack."

We winced.

"I have only to push this lever and you fall to your very painful doom."

"Bugger that," said I, and shot him. The zombie ape creatures, bizarrely attuned to their environment, sat and read newspapers. "Now I suggest we walk out very slowly, careful not to antagonise these mutant apes."

We calmly left, each resisting the urge to run. When we left the building, we must have covered several miles in quick strides before either of us spoke.

"On the plus side, the evil mastermind behind this is dead." Holmes spoke slowly.

"That's true," I agreed.

"One slight drawback is that his creations live on, in abundance. Plus, they've formed a government," he conceded, "so at any moment those creatures may descend on passers by to feast on their brains, and it will all be legal."

"Not one of your greatest successes," I offered. "But at least look at the bright side. They may not get re-elected."

Afterword

Holmes is a twat.

A Scandal in Burnley

To Sherlock Holmes she is always *that* woman. He never used any other name for her, except some unsavoury ones, but beneath his rancour ran a seam of unfaltering regard.

I have rarely heard him mention previous cases, save in recounting exaggerated victories in a most self-congratulatory manner. She, however, was afforded a rare mantle of respect.

In his eyes she was his cardinal foe, his finest adversary. Of the many wily opponents to best him over the years, her name achieved highest accord.

Not that he fell in love with her. All emotions were abhorrent to his cold, precise mind; except for pride, sloth and envy, which he had some time for. The others were unknown to him, except perhaps for vanity. Avarice was also a favourite.

Love for him was a distraction, a weakness for narrower, more fickle lives. He always claimed that such feelings were for those less dedicated, that his practice of science and detection came first. Whatever truth may lie behind this sentiment, it is sure that Ethel Adler was for him the most notable and respected of her sex.

At the outset of this matter, I had seen little of Holmes. My practice had grown busier and I had married, settling down into a domestic routine that brought me great happiness, although it was a world away from living with Holmes.

My new wife, indeed, had intimated on several occasions that the great sleuth would not be a welcome guest in our house. My home-centred life did not lead me to challenge this opinion, seeing as I could see how one who shot up the furniture, feigned death when it was his round and played the violin like the devil torturing a maestro may well be considered something of an imposition.

We had resolved not to mention the slight problem of the undead. It was not one of Holmes' greater successes, and even ranked as among his most dismal failures, although thwarting the mastermind with a bullet was satisfying. I was unsure as to what the future would bring, as the large gangs of marauding corpses did offer something of an unsettling prospect.

Owing to the fact that I had left some of my effects at Baker Street, I ascended the stairs to my old lodgings in order to retrieve them. I found Holmes buried in his books. I knocked on the uppermost volume.

"Come in," he invited.

I dislodged the impeding tomes with a kick. My esteemed friend shook himself slightly and dredged some minor instincts of sociability from his Bohemian soul.

"Watson, a pleasure to see you," he muttered unconvincingly. Clearly the fierce energy of his sharp nature was at its most ill attuned to company, his recalcitrant mind engaged elsewhere with matters to which my company was not pertinent.

"I was in the area, and remembered several items of my effects were still here."

"Ah, do not tell me!" He spoke urgently, then closed his eyes the better to use his remarkable faculties. "It is the old razor blade you have favoured since your army days, and the marble bust of Wellington you used to throw at creditors. Correct?"

He opened his eyes and looked at me like an amateur conjurer devoutly hoping some trick had worked.

"No. I remembered a sandwich I left behind the sofa. Ah, here it is," I brightened considerably, as fine ham should never be wasted. I chewed merrily, bidding him talk. "So, what have you been doing?"

"As you see, the rooms are a hive of activity." They were too, unlike him. The place was brilliantly lit, with many piles of papers, files and volumes dotted around like eccentric pillars. His long sparse form began perambulating with the order of his thoughts, and a damn weird sight it was, too.

His rapid, eager pacing and keen gaze was a surprise. To me, who knew him far better than most would care to, this told its own story. He had found a case worthy of his abilities, and this had propelled him from his torpor to grasp the challenge. I rang the bell for the housekeeper, asking if there were any spare revolvers I could borrow.

"You have a case, I take it?" He threw over a telegram, which fluttered to a rest on the table, and followed it with his cigar case. Absent-mindedly, I put the telegram in my mouth and lit it as I set out to read one of Havana's finest.

"Watson!" cried he. "How many times have I told you not to burn evidence?"

"None," I rebuffed, hotly insulted. "It is habitually you that incinerates the clues."

"The matter is of little relevance," he muttered. "As it happens, there is a trifling affair that I am engaged in, which you may find absorbing."

His manner was not effusive. It rarely was, but I think he betrayed some gratitude at having company. Indeed, he looked over at me and bestowed one of his rare smiles.

"Marriage suits you," he observed. "I believe you have put on fourteen and a half pounds since last I saw you."

"Forty two," I corrected, patting the old tum.

"Is that so? A trifle less, I would have said. And you did not tell me you intended to return to work as a doctor."

"I did not, so how did you know?" I asked, genuinely impressed.

"You know my methods," chuckled he. "I deduce from what I see. The nitrate smear on your left forefinger, the slightly worn instep on your shoe and the faint odour of chloroform told me as much. Also, the big red cross and flashing light on your bowler."

I groaned, for I had forgotten the hat. Holmes continued showing off like a ponce. He stood before the mantel, his spare form silhouetted by the flame.

"I deduce, I observe. How else would I know that your wife has a spaniel called Perky, your neighbour Mr. Mitchell gets excited by Penny Farthings and there is an old toothpick crammed into the left side of your chimney?"

I rolled my eyes and played along. It was the only way we were going to get to the plot this side of Christmas.

"Why, Holmes, this is devilry! Bless my soul, how could

you have known that?"

"It is in the nature of what I do," he rattled on, blowing smoke. "What appears to you abstract and impossible is, in fact, simplicity itself." He smiled quietly and rubbed his hands together.

"Great Scott, you certainly would have been burned at the stake had you lived a few centuries ago," I stated, privately wishing the same was still possible. Then the smell of burning cloth met my nostrils and I saw a few telltale wisps of smoke emerging from Holmes' jacket.

"Your coat's on fire," I informed him, as somehow it had escaped his great perceptive faculty.

He flapped out the flames with an oath, and I was relieved that the forthcoming lecture on detective work was interrupted.

As he spluttered incredulity there was the piercing sound of carriage wheels ploughing through stacked cardboard boxes and skidding to a halt against the curb. Holmes whistled.

"A man of some impetuosity, I would say," observed he as the speeded up sound of footsteps racing up the staircase met our ears. A rapid knocking followed.

"Leave him wait a moment, the better to prime his anxiety. For if I am not mistaken," here he was looking wistfully out of the window, "that is the carriage of a most wealthy gentleman. I'll wager the steeds have that wonderful 'new horse smell' still on them. Get me the extra large pockets, Watson, for there's money to be made from this case."

I was about to fetch Holmes' special cash holders when the door flew open and a giant of a man stood without.

"Perhaps I should leave the two of you," I suggested, for the new arrival gave the impression of being both very perturbed and also well muscled.

"Not at all, Watson. I shall need my chronicler. Besides, things may need lifting."

The very tall and broad man walked in slowly, having surveyed us both with a grave stare. His physique was that of a demi-god, but his countenance was stern.

His dress was lavish in a way that could be considered bad taste. Also, it was surprising to find such a burly man wearing a dress. Upon closer examination I discovered it was an elaborate silk wrap, covering a well-cut fur coat. He stood in tall leather boots, clearly of the finest quality, and waved a broad brimmed hat about as he spoke. It was close to a pirate costume, but I chose not to mention this to the clearly very powerful visitor, lest he smash my face in.

The tickets for The Rocky Horror Picture Show made Holmes wonder what was under the visitor's coat.

"You received my note?" His curt bass voice had a strongly

marked Germanic accent.

"I did indeed." Holmes reached into his coat and produced a note. "It said that I would be consulted by a foreign dignitary who would conceal his identity while bringing a matter of enormous importance."

"That is true," confirmed our visitor, who produced a mask and put it on. "This way you will not recognize me." Given that we had already seen his face this seemed a little pointless, but Holmes' clients are often cretins.

"Please sit down," offered Holmes. "This is my friend and chronicler, Dr. Watson, who often helps with my cases."

"You will be assured of the need for discretion?" our visitor asked me, his deep voice somewhat muffled by the mask. I inclined my head gravely, a man of pith and momentum. I can do impressions.

Our guest began with his tale.

"You should address me as the Count Von Stramm, a Bavarian nobleman. I must insist on the utmost secrecy for the period of one year. After that, it is irrelevant. At this very moment it is of such weight that it may well have an influence on European history."

"I shall say nothing for twelve months," I assured him solemnly.

"Nor I," added Holmes.

"You must forgive the mask," continued our unusual guest, oblivious. "I act for another, a great personage who wishes even his agent to remain anonymous. I may state that the name I have given is assumed."

"That much was clear," stated Holmes, lying smoothly.

"The situation is most delicate, and precautions must be taken to ensure the stability of a great reigning family. To be direct, the circumstances involve the great House of Ormerod, hereditary kings of Bavaria."

"I had also deduced that," Holmes offered nonchalantly, sitting back in his chair with his eyes closed. I held up a flashcard with 'Bollocks' written on it. Our visitor nodded sagely.

I flicked a peanut at the great detective, which pinged off

his head. He stirred at once in the wrong direction.

"Enough!" cried out guest, and took off his mask. "I am Rotwang, King of Bavaria, and up to my neck in shit. Any more farting about with this dignified, imperial matter and you get a smack in the kisser, is that clear?"

Holmes shrank slightly at his imposing guest, and smiling ingratiatingly.

"If your Majesty would be so good as to state your case," he invited, "I would be most anxious to assist you."

"In brief the facts are these. Five years ago I was engaged upon an incognito state visit to England."

"An incognito state visit?" Holmes looked confused.

"I was looking for a palace on the English Riviera, and was told by a minion that Burnley was the place. I later had him flogged for sarcasm. However, in the receipt of this knowledge I went in search of royal quarters. I concealed my true identity in the hope of securing a bargain.

"When I arrived, it became clear that Burnley was not the intense paradise my associate had described in such lyrical terms. There weren't many gondolas, it wasn't by the sea and the town being on fire didn't help.

"I did, however, meet an intense beauty. Her name was Ethel Adler, and she introduced me to many pleasures, most of which haven't been invented in official Victorian parlance. Suffice it to say, my eyes were crossed with pleasure and I walked with a stoop for no little time.

"We fell for each other madly, and it seemed our lives would be forever entwined. How wrong I was," he tailed off sadly.

"Look her up in my index, Watson," Holmes uttered as he closed his eyes. For many years he had collected a great many articles referring to various matters of interest, all subject to his own bizarrely idiosyncratic approach. In fact, it was difficult to name a subject or a person on which he could find information.

This was in part due to Holmes' slightly irregular filing system, and thanks to this I found Ethel Adler between Corbett, the haddock burglar, and Mertoni, the drive by night opera singer. I was surprised to find it at all, and handed the file to my celebrated colleague.

"I see," muttered Holmes, flipping through the pages. "Born in Leicestershire in 1858, she trained at La Scala, studied at the Sorbonne and appeared at the Imperial Opera of Wigan – a signal honour. She retired after being chased off the stage by enraged cattle."

"Her life was a picture of dedication," our guest offered sadly.

"Hum! Did you secretly marry?"

"We did not. Our affair ran its course, and I thought no more of it."

Holmes crossed his legs and looked thoughtful.

"Then where, precisely, lies the difficulty?"

"She plans to ruin me."

"How? With a brick?"

Our guest passed a hand over his wearied brow.

It was true, her singing had got worse.

"Perhaps you'd like to bang your head against the wall now?" I ventured quietly. "Might save time later."

58

"An excellent idea," he confirmed. The consternation left his face and was replaced by a look of regretful nostalgia as he attempted to explain.

"I am shortly to be married to Claudia Lurrman von Brunswick-Saxonberg, youngest daughter of the King of Scandinavia. You may know the strict principles of her family, who eschew all forms of pleasure, including music, smiling and colours. She is herself a picture of modesty. The tiniest suspicion of impropriety on my part and the engagement will be at an end."

The noted detective pondered for a moment.

"As your Majesty is a foreign head of state, surely the matter could be assisted by the government?"

Our burly visitor bridled, his face visited by an eager pang of resentment.

"I have been in touch with Sir Kenneth Knackers, Minister for Foreigners Screwing Around. In the first instance he sent around a messenger with a vial of penicillin, a list of recommended doctors and some liniment called 'Nobeeze.' It was a most bizarre experience."

"I can well imagine. Did you clarify your situation?"

"I did. He said he was powerless to assist. I think that, under the pompous flatulence of his exterior, he considered me some species of free-roaming sybarite."

Holmes rose from his chair, strolled over to the cigarette box and offered one to our guest.

"I fear perhaps the danger is being exaggerated. How, pray, can the truth of your affair be proved?"

"My distinct handwriting." He held up a sheet covered in crayon.

"That may be imitated," assured Holmes, looking perplexed.

"My personal note paper?"

"Forged."

"The seal with my family crest?"

"Stolen."

"My picture?"

"Bought."

"A photograph of my arse, mooned in scurrilous rebuke to a football team? With Ethel grinning into the camera and holding a lighter to my cheeks?"

"Ah, that is awkward. I take it those are not on sale to the general public? No, quite. Then your Majesty is indeed fucked. By which I mean to say, your conduct could have been more discreet."

"Love made me do stupid things. Luckily the tattoo will remain undiscovered until the marriage."

Holmes clasped his hands behind his back and looked grave, as he often does when encountering serious difficulties that only serve to increase his price.

"This is a grave development. If I may say so, your Majesty has been indiscreet."

"I was young, a mere prince. I am only thirty now."

"How can this adventuress best play her hand?"

"She has mementos of the affair. I can scarcely deny their authenticity. However, Miss Adler has taken a house in London. We met there briefly. I was invited round, but to my dismay found her fury without equal."

Holmes paused for a moment, drawing heavily on his cigarette.

"As I see it, the chief problem lies with the photograph. It must be recovered."

"Attempts have been made to recover it. They have all failed. Nor is the article for sale, at any price. Enquiries have been made. It occurred to me she may have discarded the trifle in a fit of pique, and my servants attempted to drain the Thames, with straws."

"Were their efforts met with success?"

"No. Only a great many trips to the toilet."

Holmes gave a light laugh, to the visible chagrin of our visitor. "It is quite a challenging problem," observed he.

"My fiancé will break it off if that photograph surfaces," fumed Rotwang.

"How painful for you," Holmes muttered absent-mindedly. Our guest glared at him. His expression clearly said he felt it was time for Mr. Fist to visit the Teeth family.

"And Ethel Adler?"

"It is a grim matter, for her blood is fiery. She possesses a nature so ruthless the Mafia ask her for tips on dealing with late payers."

Holmes winced.

"If you cannot resolve the matter, she assures me she will make public the photograph, complete with the shorts I was wearing, verifiable by the royal arseprint. She will do it, too, of that I am sure. She has a heart of ice, a soul of concrete and her feet are made of Lego."

I saw my colleague's countenance darken, a flicker of determination shining in his eyes.

"Perhaps she has not yet tangled with Sherlock Holmes," he proclaimed, rather optimistically hoping our new client would be impressed. He, with some effort, concealed his amusement.

"I gather she plans to disgrace me the day my betrothal is announced. That will be Thursday."

"Ah, then we have three days," Holmes muttered.

"Well observed!" offered our distinguished guest, clearly wanting to spend some quality time booting Holmes in the privates. "I can see you are a rare detective indeed."

"You are too kind," my celebrated friend purred smoothly. I have often wondered whether he was being diplomatic when ignoring such remarks, or if he was genuinely oblivious. "I assume you will be residing in London as I make my enquiries, no doubt keeping yourself in some style."

"Certainly. You will find me at the Clapham Motel under the name of the Count Von Stramm."

"Then I shall be in touch with news of our progress."

"If you please. The matter will be in my constant thoughts."

"Then, as to the financial angle?"

"You have *carte blanche*."

"Impressive."

"I tell you that I would give one of the provinces of my kingdom to have that photograph."

"And for present expenses?"

The King took a heavy leather bag from under his cloak and laid it on the table, where it rested with a lucrative clink that pulled at my senses.

"There are two hundred pounds in gold and three hundred in notes," he intoned impressively.

Holmes scooped up the dosh and handed him a receipt for twelve pence.

"And Madam's address?"

"34 Suspicious Person Way, Temptress, Nr. Possible Red Herring."

Holmes took a note of it.

"One other question," asked he. "Was the photograph a cabinet?"

"No. It was a photograph." His Highness rolled his eyes, and gave me a look that said, very clearly, Shit.

"I shall wish you a good night, your Majesty. I am confident that soon there will be news for you." Our valiant guest poked Holmes in the eye and left with a sneer. I waved him a cheery farewell, saying to myself that there was clearly lots of good in him.

Holmes reeled at me, one hand clasped over his throbbing peeper.

"Good night, Watson," he added, as the wheels of the royal carriage rolled down the street. "I have work to do. If you will be good enough to call to-morrow afternoon at three o'clock I should like to chat this little matter over with you."

"I will be out until then," said I. "I have a great many rich patients who are close to death, and my duty to them is clear."

Pausing only to eat a couple of heavy meals, I picked up my portable will forging kit and left.

I awoke late, having been out on call until the small hours. I was informed that Holmes had left early in the morning and was yet to return. Having breakfasted, I made myself comfortable beside the fire to wait until he'd finished detecting.

I was intrigued to see how the matter would progress. While the case held none of the more sinister elements of Holmes' regular business, it held strange fascination. The ruin of a great and noble family was in the balance, and that was bound to be a laugh.

Earlier in the day Mrs Hudson had laid out a makeshift repast for us on the sideboard. She left saying that she couldn't stand the narrative and was out at bingo until the matter was solved.

It was close upon four when the sitting room door opened. I expected this was Holmes come with news of the plot, so I put aside my novel and looked up. A drunken, scruffy groom entered the room. He was hairy and side-whiskered, with a face flushed from dissipation.

He grunted at me and went over to the desk, rifling through the drawers and pocketing items of value. Flipping me off with the type of rude hand sign that has yet to be invented, he left with an oath.

I was marvelling at Holmes' ability with disguises when he himself stumbled into the living room, his false moustache stuck to his sleeve like Velcro. Realising we had been burgled, and that my friend's considerable detecting ability hadn't found the simplest trace of the burglar's presence, I rolled my eyes heavenwards, wondering what heaven might be thinking if it happened to look down.

"Holmes, you thundering arse!" I roared, for the miscreant had left with my favourite gentleman's reading periodical, *Naughty Ladies Get It On With Badgers*, several paragraphs of which excited me hugely. "That petty villain got the better of you, and you were supposed to be onto him."

"Are you suggesting I get things the wrong way round?" asked Holmes indignantly, as he helped himself to a mug of cake and a slice of tea. I watched in silent scorn as the liquid slopped over his hand as he tried to lift it from the plate. One born every minute, I said to myself.

"We have no time for refreshments," he declared a little sheepishly. "I have an address here which ought to repay visiting. But first, a little word on your attire." I looked down at the dour brown suit with the egg stain motif, and cocked a quizzical eye at Holmes.

He was very protective about his stash of 'gentleman's reading' material.

"It is vital we create the very best impression today. We are to look rough, poor and suave – a bizarre combination I agree, however a necessary one. Be sure you are well armed. As you know, I have a network of informants around the city. I gather this scourge, strange though it is, has the tendency to attack the grand houses. They do so at random, quite mercilessly."

"Bless my soul. Have they no respect for rank, or is this because they get a better quality of dinner there?" I had no idea if rich folk taste better. Possibly this unholy plague just enjoyed chewing on the wealthy.

"I have no idea, but we must leave, Watson, and with all haste," said Holmes, and for some reason swept imperiously from the room.

Some time later, and more than a little nonplussed, I sat in the back of a hansom cab with my colleague. I was wearing my oldest, most frayed suit, one that dated back a good many years and not a few inches around the waist. It pinched my entire body all over, with my ears growing a goodly size at the amount of squeeze being employed.

My colleague, however, was in a rare and jovial mood. The cab ride over saw him making minor adjustments to his attire until he was completely satisfied. We were, I gather, set to cut quite a dash. I had scant idea of his purpose, nor of my role in his great game.

Our cab stopped several streets away from our final destination, lest we should be spotted behaving out of character.

"We will alight here, thank you, driver," Holmes called, before neatly stepping from the carriage and walking swiftly away.

"Here, what about my blooming fare?" he called after us as we trotted off at full speed.

"What's the plan?" I gasped as we rounded the corner and headed for our destination at a more sedate pace.

"Simple. We visit Ethel Adler and introduce ourselves into her affections."

"Both of us? I know the King was a big chap, and the two of us might be required from a certain viewpoint, but won't she find it a bit unusual?"

Holmes gave a quick, sharp laugh.

"I fear you spend little time studying the opportunistic nature of London's criminals," he observed indulgently. "It is a common occurrence for such rough opportunists to operate in pairs. One plies the affections of his trade while the other deals with distractions, such as maiden aunts, girlfriends or suspicious butlers who wanted to trouser the valuables themselves."

"Then surely she will be on her guard for such a practice?"

Holmes shot me an urgent look.

"What do we not mention, Watson?"

"Holes in the plot," I recited sheepishly, like a naughty boy called upon to repeat the rules.

"Quite so. We shall worm our way under her guard, then force her to tell us where the photograph is. She, naturally, will be hopelessly in love, no doubt willing to do anything to please."

"Right," I said very slowly, drawing out each syllable.

We turned into the path of a lavishly appointed house. Holmes stood forward with a dandified manner and knocked loudly on the door. There was a brief pause, following which the door creaked open. Standing before us was a butler, a stout embodiment of servile dignity.

"How may I help you?" He spoke in the elegantly respectful tones of one paid a pittance to open doors and kiss arses. He winced as he spoke, as if talking to Holmes was something of an indignity. I could readily sympathise.

"A hearty afternoon, my good man," drawled Holmes in his best attempt at a libertine's manner. "I need to speak to the lady of the house with all speed."

"I shall inform her Ladyship you will be talking quickly," said he and buttled off. After a brief wait the door opened. An elderly woman came out and peered at us both with an understandable air of mystification.

"Hello. Can I help you?" she enquired in friendly, grandmotherly tones. "Perhaps you should try speaking slowly?"

"Her Ladyship is unused to those whose conversation is conducted rapidly," explained the butler, his air of resignation apparent once more. With my trained medical mind, I could at once see the traits of one who resents his position, and who strikes back by subtly despoiling the teapot.

"Coleridge is most thoughtful," she smiled kindly. "He does look after me. Mind you," said she, leaning forward in a conspiratorial fashion, "his tea tastes bloody awful."

Holmes considered his reply for a moment, while our attention was drawn by a small, perplexed looking animal. It was pawing at the window, with a most peculiar aspect to its appearance.

"Oh, how delightful!" the elderly woman cooed. "Doesn't Mr. Figgis look adorable dressed as the Duke of Wellington?"

"I said 'Have you any clues,' not shoes!"

Upon closer inspection I was surprised to see that the animal was indeed wearing some bizarre apparel at the expense of its dignity. Holmes was revolted.

"Madam, I deduce that Mr. Figgis hates you, and is making a mental note to defile your slippers at the earliest opportunity."

Holmes was distracted by the cat, while my attention was more taken with the butler being eaten by a snaffling winged homunculus behind her. The animated corpse tucked into him with delight, strands of flesh flying about the air as the poor man was devoured.

It was clear that Holmes' incomparable mental faculties had started earning their keep, for he reached out to pull the lady of the house to safety. I was trying to get a clean shot at the beast while he was doing so, but the creature pounced on Mr. Figgis' unfortunate owner.

"We must get this woman to safety," cried Holmes a little too late, as the door slammed shut with a spray of blood and false teeth.

"This is calamitous," griped he. "I have lost a client. Before the bill is settled!"

I urged him to relax, and remember he was British. He brightened at this, and immediately sat in a deckchair in a pair of Union Jack shorts, a handkerchief upon his head and swigging from a can of lager.

"That wasn't quite what I had in mind," I had to say. "Still, while this poor woman met her fate at the hands of the ungodly, at least there was only one of the brutes."

I eyed the door fearfully, revolver in hand, lest the fiend should escape and devour us.

"Zombies!" Holmes belched. I turned around, my jaw gaping with the horror of the vicious spectacle before us. Flying through the air was a fleet of undead simian diners, and they were heading straight for us. I surmised they had come straight from the Houses of Parliament, judging by the blood stained pages of law fluttering at their heels as they flew. Despite the rigours of the deceased flighted monkey transmogrification process, they were still clad in tattered vestiges of their expensive suits.

Their leader took pride of place in a V shaped flock of seven. With an ever-ready aim, I got him straight through the monocle. He plunged from the sky with a hideous shriek and landed on the cat. The others headed straight for us, their bloodlust increasing visibly at the loss of their leader.

Ever mindful of the dignity of an English gentleman, we both dived into the hedge. Holmes reached into his coat and produced a broom handle with an egg whisk on the end. At the other end was a handle wired to the mechanism, to turn the rotors with his fingers at a safe distance from the teeth of the undead.

They landed close to us, clawing at the foliage in a bid to dine on detectives. Holmes was poised, a cool and deliberate figure, clutching his tool of death as he waited for the moment to strike. A likely candidate stuck its ignoble, snarling head through the leaves, snapping its feral jaws, hungry for blood.

Holmes plunged his bizarre, home fashioned weapon into the head of the marauding snaffler, its broken, blood-stained teeth grinding with the appetite for a kill. The zombie's eyes bulged as its cranium was entered, and my esteemed colleague whirred grey goo out through its ears.

"Brain omelette, bitch!" Holmes shouted.

"For God's sake, Holmes," I yelled in some consternation. "This is the Nineteenth Century. We don't use phrases like that for about another ninety years."

The onslaught was brief and savage. Our cunning ruse of diving into the hedge – certainly not a spur of the moment action to save our skins – had thrown them into disadvantage. They could not overrun us due to the thick vegetation.

The next creature to attack found himself momentarily trapped by the branches, hissing and biting in its frustration. I crammed my revolver barrel up its nose and pulled the trigger. Its eyes rattled and rolled for a moment, then it drooled quietly back into permanent death.

We fought them off one at a time. They thrashed and chewed their way through our cover, and we dealt with them as they came. Holmes' brain scrambler proved every bit as effective as my service revolver, and soon their terror came to an end.

Disentangling ourselves from the hedgerow that had proved such handy cover, we noted the decimated corpses with satisfaction. They were all dead, save for one dignified looking type. Despite having the sartorial disadvantage of being deceased, was sat quietly nibbling a severed leg as though it were a chicken wing. He was greatly enjoying this, and behaved as if it were a picnic.

Perhaps there was still some element of humanity to these strange beasts, I thought to myself as I blew his brains out.

Holmes was consulting his notebook, unmoved by the carnage surrounding him. Now that the recent threat of digestion by these pillagers was no more, he was once again the model of reason. Peering through his magnifying glass, he checked his notes and studied one particular page intently.

"As I have begun to suspect," he informed me. "This is the wrong address."

We set off for Ethel Adler's house, looking somewhat less dapper than previously. Our sojourn into dispatching the undead had taken its toll on our appearance, for we had splashes of blood and brains on our best clothes. Holmes had a sprig of hedgerow sticking in his hair. I had an eyeball on my lapel which just wouldn't shift.

At the better London addresses, it is never easy to make a good impression while looking like an abattoir. My noted friend was commenting on the matter as he squeezed blood out of his Deerstalker.

"I fear this will not help our plans," muttered he as we made our way up the right path. The house was truly impressive. Miss Adler was no longer engaged to some truly minted regal Teutonic giant, but from the size of her house, it was clear she wasn't short of cash.

The grounds were extensive, and we had a long walk up the drive. As we neared the main building, sounds of dignified enjoyment met our ears. When we got nearer, it became clear that some social event was underway.

"This is astounding, Watson. Despite the recent carnage of less than a mile away, this garden party is continuing uninterrupted. There's a fine spirit that hasn't left us."

A variety of guests were mingling, enjoying fine wine, nibbles and elegant conversation, save for one who was stood on the veranda and pissing through the open French windows, steadily filling a vase on the table.

During his leaner years, Holmes made a living modelling garden furniture.

We mingled discreetly through the assembled company until we identified Miss Ethel Adler. I was expecting a ravishing beauty and wasn't disappointed. The woman stood before me was indeed stunning. Fashionably dressed, tall and elegant, she regarded us with a languid stare. My celebrated colleague began his brilliant plan.

"My God, you're beautiful! Take my hand, run away with me. I'll ravish you senseless and write sonnets about how great your arse is."

I blinked with astonishment, for Holmes is usually aloof in matters of the heart. He seldom has any regard for women, unless it's Saucy Marigold from the pub at the corner of Baker Street. Yet here he was, conveying the impression that he had the sexuality of a delinquent baboon. It was an improvement, I must say.

Miss Adler was, unsurprisingly, somewhat taken aback. He took advantage of the pause to spring a calling card on her.

Mr. Sebastian Hotly-Soughtafter, Services to genteel ladies a speciality it read, with *Pelvis like an oiled hinge* written on the back. She looked at the card for a moment, then considered my friend and his jaunty demeanour, which was something at odds with the gore on his clothes.

Having considered the matter, Miss Adler looked Holmes straight in the eye.

"I will speak honestly, Mr. Hotly-Soughtafter. Your charming words have set my heart fluttering, but you are covered in blood. And I notice you have a brain-spattered egg whisk on the end of a stick in your coat. As I don't usually date weirdoes ..." The corners of her mouth turned down as she was clearly disparaging his suit.

"Madam, madam," Holmes' voice took on a gently beseeching quality. "Surely you can understand my desires?" He continued with the charm offensive. Recognising the importance of playing my part, I adopted a sleazy smile and stuck my crotch forward.

"Is my craving for you so strange?"

As Holmes continued his ribald wooing, Miss Adler pursed her lips.

"Perhaps you will think me vain, but of late I have received few compliments from gentlemen. I wonder has the passage of time dimmed my charms. I ask you, sir, have I lost my figure?"

"Certainly not. Why, if anything, there's more of it," purred Holmes indicating her hourglass outline with a dapper wave. She punched him square in the jaw with a beautiful right that would have pleased a prizefighter. Holmes staggered back a step, twittering birds circling his head.

She cursed him with many robust expressions, beckoning for her head gardener to lend her a stout boot, the better to kick him in the arse.

"You bleeding great self fancying fart of a detective."

Holmes was busy rearranging his face, which was still juddering.

"You knew? All this time you knew that I am the noted investigator, Sherlock Holmes?"

"Yes, of course."

Holmes looked taken aback, blanching slightly at this affront to his great intellect, such as it was.

"And you knew I am here on a case?"

It was Miss Adler's turn to look surprised.

"No, I had no idea. I assumed you were trying it on. At one point many gentlemen called round to present their compliments and slip me one. This hasn't occurred at all recently, however. I thought you were exploiting the matter."

"You have been less popular than usual?"

"Indeed. I thought it was a little bizarre, but attributed it to an incident when one of our builders whistled most inappropriately and got drool all over the front of my dress. I had him flogged for chauvinism." Off Holmes' quizzical glance, she explained, "I like to be ahead of the times."

"Fair enough," commented he, more than a little confused. "So why the problem with the King of Bavaria?"

"There was a terrible matter in Burnley, a scandal of which I will never speak. Suffice it to say I had to leave my home and have the entire house dry cleaned. The King tried to help me, but I would have none of it."

"I am puzzled as to why your match did not last."

"Because Rotwang was a perfect gentleman, a fine and noble man, quite the soul of honour. And yet this is why I could not marry him, for his pure and chivalrous spirit frankly bored the piss out of me. Now I am betrothed to Hector, a complete bastard who spends all his free time nutting pensioners, razing orphanages and punching kittens. I am far happier."

A rakish fellow with an impeccably sharp line in facial hair appeared. He wore a slightly singed aspect and his forehead bore the unmistakeable mark of a pension book. A small cat ambled by, and his face contorted with anger. He turned on his heel and chinned it with a sweet left. The animal tottered off looking dazed.

"Well, love is a mystifying thing," observed Holmes, looking more than a little mystified himself. I was about to wish the couple well when a bizarre sound could be heard. We all paused for a moment in an attempt to discern the sound.

An intense screeching met our ears, along with flapping sounds and a low mumbled groaning of "Brains … brains!" as the feral monkey shapes fluttered over the horizon.

Our hostess spotted them first, her eyes widening with dread. Upon seeing the keen apprehension in her face, we turned around to face the impending threat.

"Inside!" screamed Holmes and ran straight through the conservatory window, leaving a broken glass outline of himself, Deerstalker, pipe and all.

His speed of movement was something of a surprise. I was accustomed to his sharp contrasts of pace, moving from months of laziness to sudden outbreaks of frenetic lethargy, but this was new.

Our hostess took an altogether more dignified approach.

"Oh dear," Miss Adler sighed with the mildest intonation of regret in her voice. "It would appear to be afternoon feeding time for our new guests. I think going into the house would be a good idea."

I could only agree, and with the deftest of footwork I bounded indoors, trying hard not to look like I was saving my sorry skin. Holmes had already burrowed his way through the floorboards and was scraping away at the concrete foundations with his Meerschaum pipe.

Many of the guests herded inside, their eager heels clattering away behind me. Sounds of pain and rending flesh could be heard, and as I looked back I could see a flurry of savage dining. A mass of crazed monkey faces scowled and glared, the absence of soul clearly visible in their wild freakish eyes.

Hector, Miss Adler's fiancé, was viscously attacked by the beasts. Several descended upon him with a great frenzy of primal bloodlust. For a brief, hellish second he geysered blood. The brutal mass of undead savaged him from all angles. One of the zombies latched itself to his upper body and flew off, dropping his head on a plate of sandwiches.

From its safe position behind a flowerpot, I could see the cat chuckling.

"Ah well, that's knackered my love life," observed Miss Adler with her mouth turned down. She had little time to reflect on love and loss, for the brutes had finished off all the guests outside and were turning their attentions on us.

We, the lucky survivors, had barricaded ourselves in, bolstering and reinforcing the locks as best we could with what came to hand. It was a shame that side of the house offered only French windows for protection, as several feet of brick wall would have come in handy.

One of the undead monkeys glared at us from outside, its mordent soulless eyes burning with an evil glow. Its wings flapped as it hovered several feet from the ground, spitting frustration at seeing second helpings inside, out of reach. While the large windows made for a fine domestic feature, they were little protection against a savage horde of supernatural death dispatchers. I only hoped they didn't realise glass was fragile.

Our hostess, having seen Hector devoured and her guests treated like a buffet, decided on action. Reaching out decisively she rang a little bell with a ruthless glint in her eye.

A few moments later the butler appeared, standing politely to attention.

"Shaw?"

"M'lady?"

"Would you be good enough to go outside and heroically do battle for our life and limb? Then, if you should survive, we'll have tea on the veranda."

"I shall do my utmost, Ma'am."

Snooty pillock, I thought. His next movements were most impressive, however. He opened a cupboard that stood innocuously by the wall, and proceeded to arm himself with a most thorough and excellent selection of weapons.

He tucked away a brace of pistols, crammed shells into a shotgun and extracted a long, lethal Samurai sword that resided inside that decorously concealed arsenal.

"Are you really going to use Great Uncle Edgar's best cigar clipper?" asked Miss Adler with some disbelief in her voice.

"I think it best, M'lady," fawned he, bravely keeping a stiff upper lip.

"Oh, very well, if you see fit. Good luck, Shaw. Don't forget the tea."

This demi-god among domestic staff strode out manfully. He swung the door shut behind him with hardly a care, the thoughtless bastard damn near giving us all coronaries as we sought to barricade it shut.

He made for a good showing. As the first of the creatures sought to make a snack of him, he blazed away. The bodies fell in quick succession as his shotgun spattered monkey flesh from the flank of one, and another creature found itself headless. The wings fluttered as the decapitated remains floated a few pointless feet before dropping to the ground.

His efforts were valiant, his skill impressive. Of course, I'd have loved to join him in his courageous fight against the undead, but I was busy guarding the ornaments. Heaven help the poor swine who tried to take them.

"Are you going to go out and fight, Dr. Watson, or just snivel about indoors, making terrible excuses?" Miss Adler asked pointedly.

I was struggling for a reply when a bonanza shriek of bloodlust met our ears. For a moment we could see nothing behind the mass of gouging undead apes, clearly greatly excited. Shreds of flesh flew high in the air, diced by clamouring teeth.

The faithful retainer was visible moments later. He was trying to maintain his dignity whilst being eaten, which isn't easy. His frenzied screams revolted our ears. The creatures were all over him, chewing and gouging at his unfortunate form. Soon enough he succumbed to the unequal struggle, collapsing in a flurry of bites, his last scream tailing off into a pitiful gurgle.

"That's most unlike him," observed Miss Adler. "He's usually a model of professionalism. What a great shame."

I could scarcely agree more, the poor man meeting such a courageous and unpleasant end.

"It is such a pity. A tragedy, even," continued she, blowing her nose delicately. "Good butlers are so hard to find."

Before anyone could respond, a letter fluttered to the floor, blood spattered and trodden with monkey paw prints. Stooping, our hostess picked it up and read the contents. A ripple of shock and grief worked through her face. Silently she passed me the letter, and I read of its contents.

Dear Miss Adler

It is with some regret that I must inform you that I have been devoured by a bizarre specie of airborne savage, who appear to have eaten my brains. Therefore it is with the greatest reluctance that I am no longer in a position to attend to my duties after the fashion of my recent past, which I trust was satisfactory.

Hoping this letter finds you well and undigested,

Your obedient servant,

Harold Shaw (deceased).

PS The kettle should have boiled by now.

PPS Aaaargh! My head!

Miss Adler spoke first.

"Bugger!" she said. "Now I'll have to make the tea."

We live in lackadaisical times, I found myself thinking. If such a heroic death could go unmarked, it doesn't say much about our values. Is it any wonder I saw an old lady being mauled by chimps in a public library the other day?

I helped myself to a large whiskey from one of the decanters, silently toasting Shaw and his thoughtful habit of writing goodbye letters while being guzzled.

Several of the guests joined me, although there was a tinge of hysteria in their manner and the booze didn't last very long.

Miss Adler did not look too thrilled, and indeed, which hostess likes to tell her guests that most of them have been eaten?

Holmes beckoned her to one side, his manner now that of his regular countenance. He whispered in her ear, and she in turn gave him her full attention, speaking in a low fashion. A few quiet exchanges passed between them.

His enquiry successfully concluded, Holmes indicated that we should leave. I reached into the gun cupboard and stocked up. Outside, we saw that Shaw, that brave soul of a butler, had done good work. Most of the fiends were dead.

The occasional discarded limb, sat miserably amid smears of blood, was all that remained of the unfortunate guests. It was a grisly reminder of the dank evils visiting England, and did our nerves no good whatsoever.

The journey back was a long and bloody business. Little of this was to do with the flying zombie death monkeys. Most of them had returned to Parliament after Big Ben struck for the afternoon session. No. We just got in a lot of fights.

I for one was in excellent spirits when we returned to Baker Street. My heart was warmed by the fact that London still thrived, despite its citizens being eaten at regular intervals.

Indeed, our fine spirit of enterprise still flourished, as was shown by one cheery street vendor selling genuine Mona Lisas at a bargain price. Holmes pounced on this opportunity, getting one for the flat. I bought another as an investment, only my Mona Lisa was wearing an eye patch, which made it a collector's item and even more valuable.

Holmes had arranged for our regal client to meet us at the flat. We settled ourselves down for the evening, sat with plates of food on our knees as we stared into a corner of the room, waiting for television to be invented, when the King of Bavaria arrived.

"Gentlemen, have you concluded the matter well?" asked he, stood in the centre of our lounge like a Colossus in a bungalow.

"We have," Holmes purred in his best rich client voice. "I am happy to say the matter has been resolved in a way that should please Your Majesty."

The outraged client caught up with Holmes.

"You have been successful indeed, for Miss Adler is a formidable lady."

"I agree, Your Highness. During this case I have learned one or two curious things, most notably that if there were only one sex, far fewer people would believe in aliens."

"This may well be true, but have you saved my honour and removed the threat to my impending marriage?"

"I have indeed."

The King's face showed relief. He smiled at Holmes with gratitude, and took a bejewelled ring from his finger.

"I cannot thank you enough, Mr. Holmes. Allow me to give this ring as a sign of my accord."

"If Your Majesty will permit, there is something else I should value even more highly."

"You have only to name it."

"I observed a huge sack of cash attached to Your Majesty's belt, to which I would ascribe great sentimental value."

"It is yours," offered the King nonchalantly, passing it over to Holmes, who immediately keeled over from its weight. "But I should like to know more of the matter."

We regaled the client as best we could, with a tale of how the best laid plans of Mr. Sherlock Holmes were foiled by a woman's wit, although most men and even a few household pets could have achieved the same thing. He has previously blundered around the affairs of women. I'm reminded of the riddle of the Dancing Men, an event which saw Holmes spend three weeks trying to decipher an aerobics routine.

"And the photograph?"

Holmes pursed his lips, and spoke regretfully from behind interlocked fingers.

"I regret I cannot return it to your Majesty. Miss Adler says that she intends to keep the item, forever secretly, as a reminder of your affair."

"Ah, then it is as good as on the fire."

"No. She said she's going to stick it up her arse for old time's sake."

The Pain of the Pianoforted Parts

As I recollect some of the more bizarre and unsettling adventures of Mr. Sherlock Holmes, I have at times been hampered by his private nature. This is not modesty on his part, but due to unwillingness to be singled out for revenge. Associates of those he has jailed have attempted violence upon him more than once, as have a number of clients.

This means that a number of his most intriguing cases have gone unrecorded, which is something of an imposition to a chronicler. This imposition makes it difficult for me to recount some of the more bizarre matters that have received his attention. My memory is drawn to the wretched business of the boxing canary, the whistling tramp and the regrettable matter of the drooling Prime Minister.

Recently his consultancy had fallen upon lean times. Holmes is never regular in his habits, and varies them as he pleases. The one area in which he is predictable, however, is his intense displeasure at having no mysteries to solve. A dearth of criminal cases for him to work upon was guaranteed to sour his disposition and see his conduct take on a most trying aspect.

On the mantelpiece was a deluge of telegrams, all tattered at the edges. Holmes had opened them with great anticipation before disregarding the contents at a glance. There had been a great glut of cases to do with citizens being eaten by winged creatures. So many, in fact, that we had a sign put up in the window to the effect that such matters would no longer be investigated. It was hell trying to find the right monkey.

He fell into a brown study, and could be seen whiling away many hours as he sat at his desk, deliberating over the many shades of brown he had laid out before him. He sighed piteously to himself as he studied them, and while I am normally most tolerant of his bizarre conduct, of late it had begun to cause me great vexation.

"Holmes, I really must protest." He looked up wearily, the pallor of his skin making the shadows of his eyes more pronounced. "This indolent torpor that has descended upon you is the worst yet. You've been moping away like the Dickens for an incredible time now. Surely it is time for you to develop some new interests?"

I spoke with some hint of optimism, but secretly I did not feel my words would have a great deal of impact.

"There is nothing for my mind to do, Watson," he informed me, a dull inflection in his voice. "The work my brain is designed for is absent, and this causes me no little displeasure. Every day drags along like some interminable disease working its slow course."

"Oh, shut up and have some cocaine," replied I with ill grace. It is my custom to discourage Holmes' consumption of that vile narcotic, but of late I was thinking of giving it a go myself.

A small amount of animation returned to him as he smiled for a second, and then resumed his brown study. Magnifying glass in hand, he pored over the various shades and was once more ensconced.

Our housekeeper entered the room.

"There's a gentleman anxious to see you, Mr. Holmes," she announced after clearing her throat.

"Thank Christ for that, the plot!" I exclaimed with relief. "Send it in, Mrs. Hudson, I beg you."

She inclined her head and left the room. The effect on Holmes was remarkable. His posture changed from morose and supine to one charged with rigour, his eyes now shining as though with an electrical charge.

When the door opened again, a young gentleman of average height followed our housekeeper, who presented him.

"Ta-daaa!" she said, doing her best jazz hands. Ducking the magnifying glass which my colleague flung with impatience, she left the room with a touch of hauteur. I couldn't blame her. We'd be having turd pie for dinner that night, and no mistake. I made a mental note to eat only the pastry, then returned my attention to our visitor.

When I said he was of average height, I was relating the first detail I observed. He was, on closer inspection, a fellow of singular appearance. His eyes were narrow and deep set, and gave the impression of belonging to some small animal. His nose was tapered and trim, but protruded from his face in such a way as to invite birds to land on it. His teeth were also remarkable, having a bizarre reddish tinge unlike any I had ever seen.

"How do you do?"

"I am very pleased to meet you," replied Holmes, a keen and attentive smile on his face as in one who readily anticipates a treat. "How may I be of assistance?"

"My name is Oxley Featherstone," he began, accepting Holmes' offer of a chair. He leaned forward in the manner of one readying to impart a confidence. "I must seek your advice in a matter that is both unusual and highly perplexing."

Silently uttering a prayer of gratitude, I began taking notes.

"Omit no detail," Holmes informed him, touching his fingertips together as he was prone to do when applying his greatest attention. "The tiniest irrelevance may have colossal import, so I implore you, be precise."

He paused for a moment.

"I should point out, then, that on the way here I saw no fewer than a dozen people being eaten by bizarre, ghoulish creatures intent on devouring the grey matter inside their craniums. In fact, there was a freshly eaten cadaver in a delivery man's uniform at the foot of your building."

Holmes waved his hand in a dismissive gesture.

"I can guess what that was about," he spoke derisively. "Let's focus on the important points of your case."

The young man composed himself, and began to regale us anecdotally.

"Then I shall begin with the background to this remarkable business. Whilst I am in trade myself, with investments in a variety of shipping companies, I am descended from artisan stock. Both my parents were musicians, and my maternal grandfather possessed a great gift for fashioning ornate and rarefied instruments.

"My father could play the piano with his balls, an incredible skill that saw him feted all over Europe. Indeed, on no fewer than three separate occasions he used his knackers to entertain royalty, performing from an extensive roster of the classics. The way his nuts performed Schubert saw him welcomed in the greatest of houses.

His friends all agreed, he was a tool.

"I well remember him practising when I was a boy, seeing him hunched over the keyboard, a hand in each pocket, hoicking up the material of his trousers to allow him the remarkable testicular dexterity that his art required. Fourteen hours a day he would practice, and then retire to his bedchamber, that he may rub liniment on his valuable pods."

I turned to Holmes to assess his reaction to this highly unusual revelation, but he was a picture of fixed attention, his eyes pinched in great thought. Saying nothing, I resumed note taking as the peculiar details unfolded.

"His art was in very great demand, and he travelled much of the time, visiting one notable dignitary after another. By the time I was attending university, my father's bollocks had delighted most of the great and the good of Europe. His praises rang from the highest echelons of society, and his success brought us considerable wealth."

Holmes perked up while I blew dust from the cash register.

"Tragically, his career was cut short." My esteemed colleague sagged, and I redusted the till. "At one performance, at the house of a noted Prussian aristocrat, a musical rival performed a most foul deed."

Having previously been entirely motionless, Holmes now turned his head very slightly, curious as to the new development.

"He was not popular among his peers, then, your father?"

The young man emoted with a mixture of pride and regret.

"Rivals … he had none! There was one man, though, a devil of a fellow by the name of Maximillian Heathcote, who coveted my father's glory. This Heathcote rogue made a success of himself by playing the tuba with his arse – a most difficult feat, so I am told.

"Before my father's celebrated debut, Heathcote had been greatly lauded. His success seemed assured. Now, however, his skills relegated him to a poor second place. He was a proud man, and this bridled within him. He sneaked onto the stage, as my father played a most moving piece of Chopin, and slammed the lid down on his gifted jewels."

I cringed at this most painful of tragedies. Even Holmes, habitually aloof, closed his eyes at the thunder of this revelation.

Mr. Featherstone, absorbed in the emotion of his sad tale, continued oblivious to our responses.

Walter flopped it out unobserved.

"Surgeons battled valiantly to save his talent, but alas the music was gone from his sack. He made an otherwise complete recovery. Even his voice is normal, but his balls cannot even play the merest arpeggio, much less Beethoven."

There was a silence as our guest wrestled with his emotions. He won with an arm lock, and continued.

"As he could no longer play, my father became morose. He began drinking heavily. I see him but seldom now, and hear grave reports of his health. Today, he is but a broken man. His hair is askew, his aspect wild, and a sullen resentment has descended upon him. He is a world away from the contented artisan of my youth."

The door flew open with sudden violence. A man lurched in, his face contorted. Before his eyes rolled upwards, he managed to croak out a single word.

"Bugger."

He then fell to the floor, never to rise again. A knife protruded from his back.

"At least our Tuesday afternoon murder hasn't been affected, Watson," observed my colleague.

"Very punctual," I agreed, pointing to the clock. "Good to know the mild upset caused by the living dead flying about the place hasn't disrupted things too much."

A silence descended upon the room. Our visitor appeared to be lost in thought, and I wondered if further revelations were on the way. When it became clear there weren't, and that Mr. Oxley Featherstone had finished his tale, it was down to Holmes to enquire further.

"A most unsettling matter, no doubt. But how, pray, can I be of assistance to you?"

Our client looked into the detective's face with real dread in his eyes.

"There is a sinister game afoot!" he insisted, luckily not noticing the delight which sprang into Holmes' face. "You see, my father made enemies all over Europe, not just fiend Heathcote, who shut his career off in its prime."

"Indeed so," soothed Holmes, sensing that our client was on the verge of major emotion. The tension gathered in Mr. Featherstone's face seemed a reflection on his artistic heritage, as every conceivable gathering of nervous strain pulled his face taut and stretched his reserve.

"Pray, have a cigar? These are rather special. I had them sent up from Bond Street, although the box is slightly nibbled." Holmes proffered the partly eaten box, and our client, distracted and in something of a daze, reached forward. Holmes took one himself, and for a moment or two the sitting room was silent, save for the occasional crackle of a match.

"These have a most soothing effect, I find," Holmes observed, blowing a plume of smoke toward the ceiling.

"Indeed so," agreed Featherstone, his manner mollified with fine tobacco. "I must, however, return you to the issue of my father. I mention I had not seen him for several months. Now he has disappeared."

"He is not seen for months, then vanishes?"

Oxley Featherstone's brow wrinkled, and he appeared most puzzled.

"Following his misfortune, my father left the family home and became a drunk. In deference to my mother's wishes, I sought news of him, to quieten her mind."

"Her mind was noisy?"

"It kept the neighbours awake for weeks at a time. Even in church her brain could be heard playing the drums from beneath her hat. So I made enquiries, and visited some foul dens. I never saw him on these occasions, but heard more accounts of fresh outrages.

"He made himself quite notorious, displaying the most regrettable behaviour imaginable. At one hostelry in the East End he invited all the revellers to join him in a song, then proceeded to eat the piano stool in a fit of artistic pique. The outraged drinkers wrecked the bar, and it was only by the intervention of his one remaining friend that saved him from having the piano forcibly inserted somewhere it was most certainly not designed to fit.

"I listened sadly to the account, silently wondering why the gods gave such men great talent and then saw fit to deprive them of it, and with great cruelty, to the detriment of their minds. It reminded me of Napoleon, who achieved great fame, then lost it and went about the place telling everybody he was himself. Very sad.

"Yesterday I made my habitual rounds, asking for fresh news and dreading what I might hear. It was then I heard of this most regrettable development. Nobody had a thing to report. Briefly I was heartened, thinking this represented an improvement of a most pleasing nature.

"Then I was told the news of his fate. One evening, while being thrown out of The Wobbling Vicar, a nightclub of ill fame on the Old Kent Road, he had been set upon by thugs and bundled into the back of a hansom cab, which sped away.

"My conversant pointed a finger at a shadowy figure creeping past us. It was then I saw that low fiend Maximillian Heathcote, stalking through the night air with a most unsavoury smirk upon his odious face. I was quite convinced, then and there, that it was he was he who, having destroyed my father's career, now had designs upon his life!"

I was confused by this.

"Why would the criminal be lurking about just as you learn of his crime?" I asked in all innocence. The question provoked my remarkable colleague.

"Fool, Watson! Never point out holes in the plot." For a moment Holmes was enraged, seething in disbelief at my error, then smiled again and turned back to our guest. "Please ignore idiot bonce over here. He imagines himself amusing," Holmes purred, taking a deft swipe at me with a slipper. It rebounded from my noggin as I attempted to resume my attendant manner.

"Sorry," I offered sheepishly. "One sometimes forgets oneself."

"I quite understand," Featherstone assured me. "To be honest, I thought the plot was shit as well. However, there it is."

"No no," Holmes murmured, eyes narrowed with thought. "I find this a most beguiling series of events," he added, ever the professional. "Know you anything of this Heathcote fellow's whereabouts?"

"I have no clue," our visitor confessed.

"That is where we come in," reassured the great detective. "Watson, the phone book if you please!"

"Now, tell me who did it."

Our client left, his nerves somewhat assuaged by Holmes' repeat assurances that no effort would be missed in bringing this matter to a salutary conclusion. We worked out way through the phone book and Yellow Pages, eventually finding (in the specialist section) an anal brass musician called Williams.

Having contacted his agency, we found that he was due to perform that very afternoon at a teashop near the Strand. They found it, we were informed, a most effective way of clearing the premises following service of afternoon tea.

We decided to check the matter out, but going down to the street was no longer a simple business. We took pains to arm ourselves to the teeth, taking no chances and plenty of ammunition.

Luckily, the council had been busy in dealing with the crisis. They didn't actually do anything, but we did get a leaflet through the door. Among some extremely silly advice (wearing a stiff hat like a Bowler will make it harder to eat one's brains, for example) were more common sense ideas, and these we learned from gratefully.

When we left, the streets were filled with creatures. Judging by the crimson stain on the ground, they had fed recently. There were also covered in fresh bloodstains, which supported this impression further. They were shuffling about and mercifully not flying. This made them far less dangerous, slower and less likely to attack.

I spotted a familiar face, now sadly succumbed to this plague of madness. It was Cobblers the Begger. An impoverished assistant to my celebrated colleague, whose lowly station in life allowed him access to many useful lines of enquiry that would have been barred for gentlemen such as ourselves.

"Garn," sighed he mournfully, his mouth hanging open in a graceless drool. Being undead, it would appear, does little for the suavity of one's manner.

It was with some regret that I shot him between the eyes. Cobblers had been a good assistant to Holmes over the years, and I had greatly enjoyed patronising him and booting him in the arse. A pink fluff of brain emerged from the back of his head. Some landed in the mouth of the zombie behind him, who evidently relished this unexpected delicacy.

"There, blast him, would you?" I directed Holmes, who responded with a gratifying fusillade as I reloaded. Cobblers may have died a hellish incarnation of the walking dead, but that was no reason why a complete stranger should enjoy dining on his grey matter. The offender's pulped head sprayed across a fine distance.

The zombies were stupefied by the noise. In their recently fed state they proved far less aggressive. Indeed, many of them were startled by the noise of the shots, backing away from us in something akin to a state of fear. We took advantage of this, making good progress.

A friendly voice called out as we passed. It was Lestrade, standing at the front of a dozen burly officers, all clad in special uniforms and wearing double thickness helmets. My colleague examined them, professional curiosity mingling with amusement.

"A particularly nasty plague of the undead this morning, wouldn't you say, Inspector?"

"Not to worry, Mr. Holmes," he was cheerful. "We've got the Special Zombie Unit on it." We looked at the officers behind him, all looking primed for action, although they weren't actually moving. "They're all the range at Scotland Yard, these boys. We've got plans to lead these buggers into a trap using a cunning trail of bananas."

"Are all your squad accounted for?"

Holmes smiled, pointing out one pleased looking zombie clutching a policeman's helmet full of brains. He'd collected them from the skulls of some particularly dead looking coppers laid out in a row behind Lestrade's special team of reinforced nitwits.

The enterprising brute was clearly looking forward to feasting on them later. He was to be disappointed, thanks to a vicious hail of truncheon blows which spoiled his lunch.

We left the scene directly, Holmes determined to break fresh ground on this new and intriguing matter. The next street was far less full of the undead, so we made good progress. In the hansom cab on our way over Holmes was distracted, his eyes glued to the window.

"Can I help you, old chap?" I enquired.

"Ow!" said he. "Why was there glue on this window?"

"Never mind," said I, still resenting him for slippering my forehead. "That'll teach you to press your face up against the glass and make faces at passing urchins."

Through the inventive use of my hip flask, a twig in each nostril and a certain amount of force, I detached my colleague's face from the glass. We arrived at our destination. Somewhat disorientated, Holmes reached into his pocket to pay the driver, staggered a step or two and then lead the way into the cafe.

"I knew putting glue on the windows would pay off."

Owing to something of a shortfall in my army pension, I have at times been forced to dine in less than first-rate establishments. I cannot help but wince when recollecting meals eaten, or rather endured, at places like The Stuffed Mouse or The Gastric Disaster. More than once I have consumed what might loosely be described as foodstuffs on these premises, only to regret it in the same way one might consider it foolish to try and drink the entire Thames.

This eatery looked less poisonous, but at the same time I would not care to try their offerings. We passed several patrons leaving, all looking green about the gills. I looked at Holmes, and noticed he was ducking slightly as he passed them, doubtless wishing to avoid being spattered with the end product of a regrettable encounter with what could be called dinner.

Inside, waiters were clearing tables, several wincing as they did so at the slops dribbled over the side of plates and doing the varnish no good whatsoever. A tall man in a frock coat stood at the till, looking over receipts with a glee that I deduced meant he was the proprietor.

Then my eye landed on what must surely be the gentleman we had come to converse with. He was short and portly, with receding brilliantined hair and the matter of an artisan. He was packing a tuba away in its case, and that fact, coupled with the singe marks at the back of his trousers, clearly marked him out as Mr. Heathcote, of dubious fame and even more dubious talent.

"I see our man isn't here," Holmes sniffed, his attention on a plate of soup that looked as though anyone unfortunate enough to have eaten some must surely have expired soon after.

I pointed Heathcote out to Holmes who, it was clear, was not fully over his recent experience with glue and the window of a cab. We sidled over, Holmes slipping into character as the lofty, aloof man of intellect. His acting skills are amazing, but I still think he was more convincing that time he played Widow Twankey in the Scotland Yard Christmas panto.

"Have I the doubtful pleasure of addressing Mr. Maximillian Heathcote?" he enquired with a hefty dollop of sneer in his voice. Our man straightened up, if that word can be applied to one so round.

"You address he," he replied, attempting to match Holmes in the pomposity department. I could have told the poor fool he was deluded to even try. "Why is that such an unpleasant experience, may I ask?"

94

"Oh, you see I am acquainted with a gentleman by the name of Oxley Featherstone. The surname rings a bell with you, perhaps?" Holmes was clearly in no mood for subtlety.

As the situation could well develop into a confrontation between criminal and sleuth, I discreetly reached into my coat, my hand resting on my revolver. If this arch-fiend was to turn vicious, I was resolved to shoot first, consequences be damned. I didn't survive a war only to face death in a dismal London restaurant.

Heathcote's brow furrowed. He face showed no guilt.

"Why yes, I am acquainted with the gentleman. It is a name I have not heard in a long time, mind you. But yes, I know of him."

"I see." From the way he spoke, it was clear Holmes did not share my opinion of his innocence. "Where you close friends?"

"Why no. In fact I hated him. But it was not me who caused his downfall, Mr. Holmes. Pray give me a moment of your time. I am confident I can persuade you of my innocence."

I could see my colleague was impressed with this speech. It could never be said of Sherlock Holmes that he did not listen to suspects. For one thing, their tales sometimes ended in a confession, which made his life a lot easier, even if it didn't help the drama of tales such as these. Some people have no consideration.

At the request of Heathcote we followed him to a nearby street. He lead us into a salon. It was filled with artists, the kind who frequent fashionable bistros, the better in which to imbibe heavily, catch syphilis and bemoan the artistic spirit.

We passed through the doors of Café Bolloques. It was far more impressive than our last haunt. It was a little dirty, it is true, but the fixtures inside were decadent. It was full of artisans, most of them in the throes of advanced inebriation.

"Mr. Holmes, Dr Watson, please sit with me. Allow me to tell you of my career. I gather you know how it was curtailed, but not how it was regrettably intertwined with the Great Featherstone, and the truth of the damage to his musical appendages."

He beckoned to a waiter. After the spirit of the place, the waiter sidled over with laconic resentment. He eyed us with disdain, looking as though he may start composing verse about our general shittiness at any moment.

A round was ordered, and we settled ourselves down. Despite the fine settings, the quality of the drinks was clearly lacking. Holmes sipped his pint and made a face like a fish being strangled.

"Oh look, Queen Victoria doing a strip," pointed he, and I looked aside as he poured his beer into the pot plant, which promptly withered. As I could see no sign of our great sovereign getting her kit off – unusual for a Wednesday – I could only assume that Holmes' great observational powers were once more working their magic.

It was a pleasure to sit in a more civilised locale, especially as nobody was having their brains eaten. As Heathcote began talking, a light of pleasant nostalgia entered his face.

"My history in novelty music goes back all through my life. My parents were celebrated performers in their own fields. My father could play all of Chopin on the tambourine, and my mother could play the viola with her toes."

We said nothing.

"In addition, my granny could play all of Mozart's 41 symphonies on the banjo, and Great Uncle Edgar is the Funktastic Beatbastard at Club Dagdha in Berlin."

"I see. Well, congratulations," I offered, unsure of what to say. He looked around, then gestured for silence.

"One of the reasons I come here is for the exquisite music. Listen, for this should be superb."

We paused to hear a crooner sing a delicate ballad, a moving tune that used all the notes in the musical firmament, some of them twice. I was wiping away a tear when a distant scrabbling noise caught my attention. I rushed over to the window to see what was happening, and the sight outside fair took my breath away.

Massed outside in a heaving throng of evil was a large group of lawyers. I hissed and threw stones at them, until I remembered to replace my glasses. Peering closely, I realised it was only a group of shuffling undead apes, their wings folded back as they peered in. More people joined me by the window, many outraged by the sudden apparitions.

96

"Have you no sense of decorum? Leave us in peace, you evil fuckers," yelled a distraught elderly gentleman.

"It's all right," I assured him quietly. "They aren't really lawyers."

"I'm relieved to hear it," said he, sitting down to mop his brow. It seemed that flighted ape corpses worried him less than a mob of baying solicitors gathered at the door. I could see his point.

I looked outside. Once more the zombies were defeated by the windows, staring forlornly into the glass and cramming their dazed monkey features up against the panels. From our vantage point of comparative safety, we could study the brutes. They were a most hideous sight, for such were the ravages of decay. One of the zombies had a face like a kick in the bollocks.

It was a full, perturbing collection of creatures that faced us. Only last week my celebrated colleague had found himself cornered by such an unsavoury mob of brutes, from which Holmes cleverly escaped on his customised tricycle. I was wondering what would deliver us this time, or was this the end of the road?

"Sod 'em," decided Holmes. "Somebody else will deal with it."

We resumed our seats as patrons hurled rocks and made faces at the undead army gathered at the door. It was an unusual reaction. As we sipped our drinks, the café patrons tried a variety of means of escape. My favourite was making a human catapult out of the hat stand, a large belt and the wine waiter. Admittedly, everyone who tried it died hideously, but full marks for effort.

This improvement to the cabaret improved my spirits no end, although Mr. Heathcote grew sombre.

"As you can probably tell, my fortunes have fallen distinctly. See how thin I am?" We regarded him with some sense of disbelief, as he was far from slender. Rotund, if anything. "A while ago I could have tipped the scales on a hippo. Now a gust of wind could knock me over. Well, a gust of wind that came from a hurricane." He had started sobbing during this speech, and blew his nose rigorously.

Holmes interjected, eager to stem this tide of self-pity.

"What was your downfall, Mr. Heathcote?"

His face contorted into a mask of hatred.

97

"It was vicious gossip, Mr. Holmes, nothing less!" He spoke with such passion that Holmes and I were impressed. Perhaps this man had been unjustly blamed?

"I remember the evening well."

It was a grand event in the Viennese social calendar. 1892 was a wonderful year for the social elite of the area. Wine flowed in abundance. The magnificent settings of castles and vineyards hosted many grand occasions.

I had been a massive success, my skills making me the toast of the season. Lavish parties were held in my honour, and I was feted like few before. Celebrations of my art knew no boundaries. I was presented to royals and premiers as I attended the finest events.

I was paid handsomely, happy to grow accustomed to the very best. I had servants, a gold carriage and a large entourage of sycophants to compliment me. Every merest whim was catered for.

Many beautiful women competed for my eye, although I will never understand why some people think a good display on the athletics field gives them the right to one of my peepers.

The party circuit in Europe is one that attracts great performers. No matter what feats of brilliance, daring or skill were performed, my bum tuba always carried the day. I was an artist assured of an audience, a happy man whose pockets flowed with money.

A rival came into my idyllic world. I say a rival, but I flatter myself. He immediately grabbed the admiration of all concerned. From the first day I laid eyes on him, I hated him. When I saw his celebrated feat, my heart sank to the soles of my shoes.

The first time I encountered Oxley Featherstone Senior was at the Grand Duchess DuLanier's Spring palace. This magnificent building contained only the very best. We had just celebrated her 30th birthday for the thirty-eighth time, which is one way of staying young.

I had already performed, and given it my all. In addition to being a fine event, I was also aware that my position on the roster of events was lower than usual. No longer the star attraction, I could only guess at what caused this ignominious demotion. Resolving to give Handel the rendition of a lifetime, I lowered my britches and fitted the mouthpiece to my arse and let go with a majestic display.

Muted applause followed. I was uncertain as to why there were not the celebratory whoops of my regular performances. I accepted this, however, and left the stage, wondering why my fortunes had changed.

And then he followed me, Featherstone, a preening, foppish nincompoop dressed in gaudy satins. He strutted about the place like he was the greatest thing since sliced bread, even though that hasn't been invented yet.

Excitement rippled through the palatial ballroom – which is an apt name, given his performance – and cries of 'Bravo, Maestro!' could be heard. This before he had played a note!

He greeted the crowd with a bow that was more leering flourish than dignified greeting. That over with, he turned to the piano, whipped out his tackle and produced to play Rachmaninov, using only his balls. It was a remarkable sight, as delightful to the ear as it was revolting to the eye.

Seeing this, my jaw dropped, and I realised that my great good fortune had come to an end. I grabbed a passing waiter, but this was a mistake due to my shock. Apologising, I grabbed a glass of wine and proceeded to drink myself stupid.

I do not know what occurred then, gentlemen, save that I awoke in a strange place. I over imbibed, that much I know, as a means to blot out my disappointment and envy. The strange place appeared to be a police cell.

Unaware as to how I got there, I waited quietly until summoned. No little time later I was called to the magistrate, who charged me with lewd conduct, defiling a fountain and vomiting into the top hat of a young aristocrat.

I paid a nominal fine and left the court, my recent disgrace a minor blow next to the crushing defeat to my hopes. I returned to England, and here I am.

Some time after my return, I heard of Featherstone's injuries. It was a terrible thing. Losing your music is bad enough *without having your bollocks flattened in the process. Many accusing fingers pointed my way, but I had no part in it.*

He finished his tale sadly, with the air of one recounting the singular, most terrible experience of their life. The genuine nature of his emotion left me in no doubt as to the accuracy of his tale. I, however, am not a skilled detector of human frailty. Whether or not the great faculties of my celebrated friend would find any deception in the matter, I could not say.

"Is he lying?" I hissed quietly.

"No idea," he admitted.

It is possible we were distracted with our thoughts when the next outbreak hit us. Any doctor will confirm that contamination requires delicate handling. All manner of infection can creep quietly under the most watchful nose, and this is how the next outbreak occurred.

The waiter started hissing and spitting, which I assumed was his overly sensitive reaction to a small tip or perhaps a customer asking for something of which he did not approve. Given the overall snootiness of the place, neither would have surprised me.

A yowl of feral temper left his lips, and I turned around to see the waiter fully transformed into one of the fiends. His nose had flattened into his face, his jaw had rounded and his aspect became markedly simian. More than that, he started eating Mr. Heathcote, biting into his head with hideous relish.

"Oh my God!" screamed one of the patrons. "Does that mean no more drinks?"

Guilty or not, Heathcote was being digested. It wasn't the most exact piece of deduction ever, but that couldn't be helped. The shock of this attack had me at a disadvantage, but I soon recovered myself and shot the offending waiter, something I had been wanting to do since I first laid eyes on the arrogant fellow.

His corpse lay in heap as I looked at the sorry mess that was our number on suspect. The poor, semi-eaten musician lay on the floor, gasping feebly. Holmes was concerned, immediately taking charge of the situation.

"Watson, you're the medical man. How stand his chances?"

"Not great," I was forced to admit. "You see the big hole in his head, where the brains are falling out? That's not good."

In fact, I was amazed he was still alive. He croaked feebly, beckoning us close that he may talk with his last breaths.

"I am innocent," he wheezed in agony, each syllable clearly a massive effort.

"Fair enough. One last thing. Where can we find the bad guy?" Holmes asked pleasantly.

"Little Milton," gasped he in extraordinary pain.

"Thank you," my colleague replied cheerfully.

"You get a train to Newton Liddle ... I think one leaves Victoria Station at about two o'clock."

"Thanks."

"Then you have about a fifteen minute walk ..."

"Okay."

"It's just near a small church."

"We'll find it."

He continued in this vein for some time, but we left him to it. We got back to Baker Street feeling slightly deflated. The throng of living dead were waiting outside for us, but we took advice from the council's leaflet, which told us that gorillas hate the rain.

Holmes and I put up our umbrellas, holding our hands out and looking upwards pessimistically. The zombies merely looked disapproving and let us past without incident. I wish we'd discovered this early. It would have saved us a lot of bother.

Back in Baker Street, there were several telegrams waiting for us. All of them were unopened, although one was slightly chewed. The first was from Holmes' brother.

Sherlock,

This is intolerable. Everybody in my government department has been eaten. This, however, has made work far more efficient. Every cloud has a silver lining.

Don't rush to fix this. I suppose it's an improvement.

Yours,

Mycroft

101

PS I can be found in the stationary cupboard.

The next read:

Dear Mr. Holmes,
All my officers are now chimps. I know you've always said as much, only now they really are. Trouble is, now they're doing all the paperwork. I can't keep up.
Send help.
Lestrade (Inspector in hiding)

Worse news awaited us. According to Mrs. Hudson, attacks had occurred all over London. Outbreaks of winged monsters devouring everyone they chanced across were now an everyday matter. Given this news of fresh public devastation, I could only think that life had changed permanently.

Even the newspapers had got in on the act, with the London Gimlet getting in on the act with this headline:

Read all about it! Our wonderful chimp rulers wisely eat 15 in Catford. A nation rejoices.

Bizarre how the press will spin things to appease the powers that be, I thought to myself. "Today is a good day to kick a self important friend of yours who owns a magnifying glass," read my horoscope. "Also, you will find love with Sagittarius. Watch out for disease."

"Enough with the papers, Watson. We must go to Little Milton. Have you the revolver and my spare magnifying glass?"

"I have," I confirmed, for Holmes' working habits are no stranger to me.

"Very well. Owing to the extraordinary circumstances of recent developments, I propose we leave here separately. We may well be dealing with some kind of criminal mastermind here, and for that reason, I'd rather you went first." Off my dirty look, he realised his tactless mistake. "Because naturally, my enemies would wait for me before they struck."

102

"Quite," I was diplomatic, anxious for the off.

I arrived at the station, boarded the train and found the compartment Holmes and I had reserved. My companion, however, was nowhere to be seen. I cursed myself for leaving him alone. I suspected foul play.

"So ... who pinched the table, then?"

In Holmes' stead was a man of about Holmes' age and size, but wearing a pair of plastic spectacles, with a round scarlet nose and rubber moustache underneath.

"I say, my good fellow. I believe that to be my companion's seat. I do not suppose you have seen him?"

The fellow pulled his glasses to one side, and lo! there was my friend, in a disguise that would fool his own mother.

"Not a word, Watson, I do not wish to be observed."

"God, Holmes, that's unworldly," I said, clutching my chest at the shock.

He gave a small smile of content, replaced his glasses and was once more undetectable.

We arrived at Little Milton in due course. It was a grand mansion full of Gothic features and suggestive settings. Basically it was the usual deal, creepy as hell and with no neighbours in sight. I rang the bell as my celebrated colleague settled into his adopted disguise.

A languid butler answered the door, peering down his nose at us, as was professionally required.

"Yes, gentlemen?"

"It's Sherlock Holmes for the bad guy," said Holmes, then flinched at the realisation of his own stupidity.

If the butler found this unusual, he did not show it. I wondered if the house often received such bizarre visits.

"I shall inform my master of your presence, also of your most convincing disguise." I could sense Holmes grimacing underneath his joke shop moustache arrangement. The butler left us alone for a moment. I glared at Holmes, for his blundering could have cost us dearly. He stood there slightly wilted, his manner lacking its customary arrogance.

"Step this way, gentlemen." The butler returned to lead us through the spacious hall, crammed with bizarre statues of famous figures in compromising positions. It was indeed a most unusual sight.

The butler held open a door.

"This way, sirs."

Just after he spoke, a jarring chord rang out. We walked through the tall gilded doors and found ourselves standing in a ballroom, a very grand, ornate affair. The centrepiece of the room was a lavishly decorated piano. It was a long, hand painted instrument, sitting beneath the chandeliers, which were real glass. It was all very posh.

Our client, Oxley Featherstone the Younger, was waiting for us. He was sat at the piano in a most bizarre position. His head was slumped into the keyboard, sustaining a jarring chord.

"Very dramatic," I noted with approval. "Things are looking up."

I was sure that something was wrong, but at Holmes' insistence we sat down, politely paying attention and looking as keen as any conservatoire students. Featherstone didn't move, apparently keen on following his father's example of irregular musicianship.

We sat there quietly. The great detective insisted we pay close attention lest our musical client take offence. An hour or more had passed before we realised all was not well. For one thing, he hadn't budged at all, and didn't even appear to be breathing. At first I thought it was part of his performance, but then his head began rolling forward, his tongue lolling out as his eyes gazed lifelessly forward.

Holmes, that great observer, found the root of the trouble.

"There's an arrow sticking out of his back. So, he wasn't playing the piano at all."

"I see," I said, feeling rather foolish for having applauded so enthusiastically.

A slow handclap echoed mockingly behind us.

"My congratulations, gentlemen. Poor Oxley here's been playing F sharp for the last hour, and it didn't occur to you to look? Ah well. Detectives aren't what they used to be."

We turned to face a tall, elderly figure. His face was gaunt, but not with age. It was as though a tapeworm of evil was lodged inside his system, gnawing at the vitals of his existence from within.

"As you can see, Mr. Holmes, my fascination with novelty music continues."

He was well dressed, with a gold chain reaching around his side and into a waistcoat pocket. It was his expression that was most peculiar, however. His eyes gleamed with a jubilant evil that reminded me of a snake that had been at the laughing gas, and his mouth was twisted into a grin that, try as he might, could not conceal the sadism it ill disguised.

Holmes was yet to find the power of speech. I was sure that recent events had been taking their toll on him, and such proved to be the case.

"I sent you a number of clues, all carefully selected. It was clear I had to pander just enough, to beguile your intellect and lead you to an exquisite demise."

My esteemed colleague looked puzzled. He shook the vacant expression from his face.

"No," said Holmes, his lips pursed downwards.

"Really? You amaze me. I heard you were a formidable intellect, a reasoning machine above human frailty, whose one function in life was to act like a one man science faculty. Well, if you missed them all, you truly are an arse.

I considered this a forgivable slight, given Holmes' gormless response. Plus, having known him for years, I agreed entirely.

"You also missed the trail of money I left for you? How regrettable."

Holmes had faced his nemesis with a stoic disdain that became him well, but at this revelation he began sobbing and banging his head against a table.

"And I just murdered your one lead just to make an entrance," the killer mused to himself. "Quite a waste of time, really."

My eyes wandered over to the unfortunate young man face down in the piano. Were it not for the arrow protruding from his back, the lifeless eyes and the complete absence of vital signs, it would have looked quite a refined scene of musical contemplation.

"As you have no idea about me, allow me to explain myself. I am a retired musical agent, which is how I knew Heathcote." Again he beamed a crocodile grin.

As he read the ending, the villain knew what to do next.

"I grew up in the small southern village of Willington, where we pride ourselves on our musical evenings. Twice a year great occasions of joy and feasting accompany the finest music our little community can offer."

"This was of a particularly high standard, no doubt?" Holmes pronounced in a measured tone of deduction.

"No, it was shit, but we enjoyed it hugely because of the alcohol and incest, which made for a tremendous evening. It also explains the excessive amount of body fur the village is reknown for, but that's side effects for you.

"Willington has a particular, even warped, character. It had always been my intention to live there, however I accidentally won a scholarship to impresario school. My family were adamant that I go, largely because they couldn't stand me.

"London was an amazing place for a young man used to a village of only fifty square feet. I found a rich cultural seam. A niche of artists developed most unusual approaches.

"I recall Benson, an avant garde sculptor. Instead of a chisel, he used to headbutt the marble into shape. Sooner than condemn his bizarre way, I offered him a contract. In this way did my success begin, by finding such rare talents and putting them on the stage.

"I was successful immediately. People flocked to see these bizarre feats, and my social advancement was assured. Who else could deliver such a multi-pantheoned freakshow under the guise of art? I expect a century from now, any old toss will be lauded to high heaven. Such is progress."

"So I observe," Holmes lied.

"As soon as I saw Heathcote he was, briefly, the golden boy. I signed him immediately I saw the mouthpiece of a tuba sticking out of his arse."

Lightning crackled outside, with a rolling wave of thunder adding greater menace to an already terrible scene. Death and madness reigned.

"That was fine, so far as it went. Then Oxley Featherstone Senior came along, and he was a sensation. But these things have a limited appeal. I insured his gifted testicles for a large sum, then hypnotised another musician – whose skills I had no longer had a use for – with a slice of cake."

"Cake?"

"Battenberg. The different coloured squares have a most beguiling effect when rotated correctly. Heathcote had no idea of his actions, and I became richer."

The weather was doing its bit adding to the overall menace. As the grandiose interior of the room was being erratically lit by nature's sinister electricity, I found myself getting impatient with this pompous buffoon. For one thing, I already had one of those in my life.

"Since I assume we're going to die anyway, you may as well tell us your name."

"Gentlemen, you must forgive my discourtesy. I am Valminder Ocrasto, last of a long and bizarre line that has woven a noose around many great personages throughout the ages. My parents, Lafcardio and Jizmella, took pains to instil a sense of pride in this conduct."

"I bet you caught hell at school for having a name like that," I enjoyed my little dig.

"Scarcely at all," he wiped the smile from my face. "Some of my schoolfellows did find my name amusing, for a brief while. Then they disappeared."

Well, that wiped my smile.

"Just out of curiosity," Holmes enquired mildly, "how did you plan to do away with us?"

He appeared at a loss for a moment.

"With this bow and arrow."

"Ah. You need another arrow, I think."

"True," he agreed, looking thoughtful. "I was just going to ring for my butler and have him bring me two."

"I see. The usual please, Watson," my celebrated colleague requested languidly.

"Certainly," I agreed, pleased to help, and shot him.

"Surprise endings ... who will buy my surprise endings?"

The Mystery of the Speckled Wang

On considering the cases presented over the years, it is clear that a great variety of matters have been considered. I am almost reluctant to do so again. However, my duty is clear, and so my pen must once more reluctantly scratch an effigy of one of the finest, wisest men of our time, and my assistant, Mr. Sherlock Holmes.

Thanks to the interventions of Holmes, the streets of London were safer, especially for the multitude of criminals who preyed upon the poor and weak. The latter group could not possibly afford the attentions of a top specialist like Holmes, who didn't get out of bed for less than two shillings.

The decade or so over which I studied the methods and singular life of Mr. Sherlock Holmes has presented a vast array of cases – many tragic, some trifling and at least one involving indecent exposure.

The crimes Holmes has investigated, however, fall into a more robust pattern. While a kidnapping or threat of murder would be distressing to the everyday soul, they formed his regular professional diet. Indeed he was never happier than when surrounded by clues, crimes and Scotland Yard.

From all these disparate plunges into human misdemeanours, one that stands out is the harsh and miserable affair concerning Dr. Grintle Roycott and his unfortunate nieces. Such a matter is a rarity, even for Holmes. It is only now, when the lawsuits have been settled and damages paid, that I can reveal these events to the reading public.

It was March in the year 1886 when I awoke early one morning to the unusual sight of my colleague, sat opposite me and bouncing peanuts off my head in an attempt to rouse me from my slumbers.

Being of regular habits, I dislike these being disturbed by one of his numerous eccentricities. I sat up wearily, for I like to get in my full sixteen hours before arising. Holmes was fully dressed, a slight, curious smile on his face.

"Very sorry to wake you, Watson, but there is much to be done. Mrs. Hudson has been knocked up –"

"What!" I interrupted through my haze of sleep. "Which randy old sausage did that?"

Mr. Hudson, our erstwhile housekeeper's spouse, was a gentleman of most regular habits, caused by his death some years ago. Since that regrettable occasion, he has been reliability itself and has hardly ever moved from the cemetery.

"You misunderstand," Holmes laughed, pinging another legume from my bonce. "Our housekeeper is dressed and preparing the sitting room. We are shortly to receive a visit that promises to be most fascinating."

With that my full attention had been seized, and I roused myself. The clock on the mantelpiece told me it was approaching half past six, and I set aside my vexation at the unusual hour for the anticipation of a case that suggested great interest.

Mrs. Hudson had certainly been busy in the sitting room. The regular detritus of Holmes' unorthodox lifestyle had been ordered most thoroughly. His case files, habitually in such disarray, had been tidied. I noted with approval that the death threats were placed into alphabetical order and wedged underneath the clock, which now scraped the ceiling.

"What's the occasion?" I asked in some surprise.

"I expect a visitor, and a most promising case. A telegram of some urgency arrived shortly before I woke you. I was still up from the night before, having stayed up late with the pay-per-listen boxing on the radio."

I grunted my acknowledgement of this, as I am never at my best first thing in the morning. Leaning back in my favourite armchair, I smiled cheerily at our housekeeper as she thoughtfully brought me a tray of breakfast.

I poured a cup of coffee and glanced at the newspaper. It seemed the first zombie to make a speech in the House of Lords – it wasn't long, for he just said, "Brains" – was met with applause. A tax on those who hadn't yet been eaten was announced.

Quietly blaming the government, I set about the toast and eggs with enthusiasm. Holmes watched indulgently, for I am a messy eater. He rarely made a big meal of breakfast, often preferring several pipes, a pot of coffee and the papers. Today he disappeared behind an unusually acrid plume of smoke, with the occasional rustle of newsprint the only sign of his presence.

We sat in silence, preferring to keep to our thoughts. My anticipation of the meeting could scarcely have eclipsed that of Holmes, whose rustling became agitated with tension.

The ringing of the doorbell roused me from my meditation with a grunt. A young lady was ushered in. She was uncommonly well dressed and carried with her an air of disturbance. Her face was drawn by some inner sorrow, and I could only wonder what had she heard about Holmes to cause this.

"Good morning, dear lady," I charmed, nonchalantly removing a fried egg from my ear. She graciously offered a hand, which I clasped with a respectful fervour that left butter all over her glove.

Holmes was more reserved, standing with a thin smile of welcome on his face. He ushered her to an armchair by the fire. Once she had warmed up a little, he spoke.

"It is a pleasure to see you. I am Sherlock Holmes, and this breakfast spattered fellow is Dr. Watson, my assistant and chronicler. You may speak absolutely frankly before him, as his ears are blocked with egg. I see that you still shiver. I shall pour you a cup of coffee."

"I never wear it. But it is not cold that affects me so, Mr. Holmes. It is the strange, unnatural events that have befell me which quivers my constitution."

Holmes cocked an eyebrow, his curiosity piqued by the hope of a case of weird horror, which he loves. In fact I have even known him add a 12.5% surcharge for cases that offer nothing out of the ordinary.

The young lady lifted her face towards us, and indeed lines of terror were forming. Her eyes held the haunted quality of one who lived with daily fear. Streaks of grey shot through her hair. I would not be surprised if it was recent developments that wracked her so.

Holmes' eyes flickered over her impassively, but the objective reserve of his exterior betrayed nothing.

"For God's sake, Holmes, just use the teabags like anybody else."

"You must not fear," he said soothingly. "For these events, however terrible, no matter how likely it is that you will die–"

"Holmes!" I intervened, for the young lady's face had drained of colour. "We must not increase her fears."

"Of course," Holmes replied smoothly. "We must hear all of your tale, then decide how best to proceed. You are in excellent company, for I am England's most acclaimed independent crime specialist."

I didn't like to mention that he was the only one. Not the time, plus it wouldn't help with the advertising.

"Oh Mr. Holmes," the young lady entreated. "I shall go mad if this strain continues, I know it. There is nobody who can help me, and only one who cares, and he, for all his good intentions, cannot assist.

"I was given your address by a neighbour, Mrs Farrington, who you aided last year. Won't you help here and throw some light on the eerie darkness that surrounds me?"

I thought it was pretty unlikely myself, but she continued before I could say anything.

"She mentioned that I could expect complete discretion from you."

Holmes' interwove his fingers as he recollected.

"Mrs. Farrington? Oh yes, I remember the case. Her neighbours never stole her newspaper again," he turned to me with a smile.

"Quite so," agreed our visitor. "However, at present, I am not able to pay you." Holmes' demeanour sagged. His manner had been one of an eager professional waiting to get cracking and send off fantastic reports and exaggerated bills. Then the pipe drooped in his mouth and his eyes registered disappointment.

"However, in a month or six weeks I shall be married, and then in receipt of a sizeable income," she continued, oblivious to Holmes' reaction. "Then I shall be happy to reward your efforts."

In many areas, Holmes demonstrates a reasoning capacity that would disgrace the average squirrel. Where matters of finance are concerned, however, his mind was a razor with deep pockets.

"It would … help if I knew something of your circumstances, perhaps, to begin with."

"Certainly, Mr. Holmes. My name is Helen Simpson, and I live with my stepfather in the Home Counties. My mother was one of the Saltson-Wiltbys, whose wealth was remarkable even among the plutocratic.

"Sadly, the family fortune declined, due to profligacy and intemperance." Holmes' enthusiasm waned a little, and his mouth turned down. "She married a wealthy man called Simpson who died young, when my sister and I were in our infancy. Leaving us with a governess, she went out to Calcutta, where a local medical doctor by the name of Grintle Roycott wooed her.

"He was English by birth, and had obtained his medical degree before heading out. By force of personality and some forged signatures, he built a large practice, and they married."

I had been taking notes, also drawing a caricature of Holmes skidaddling out of the British Mint with a wheelbarrow. One gets these impulses.

"Dorothy, I thought you were going to put your face on. Where is it?"

"It was not a happy union. My stepfather's temper began to make their lives very difficult, and following a local burglary he chased off all his patients with a long chasing implement."

Holmes' attention arched here, as he sensed the nub of the matter approaching.

"They returned to England after a great scandal, and it was only through paying a vast sum of money that he avoided a lengthy prison term. Taking up residence in our ancestral home should have been a welcome break from such disruptions, but it was not to be."

"His fierce disposition made itself known once more?" asked Holmes, as I drew him performing a circus act with a monkey on a unicycle.

"Indeed it did, Mr Holmes. Instead of enjoying a pleasant rapport with neighbours, there was a series of bitter rows, usually followed by violence. My stepfather is extremely strong. Once in Calcutta he floored an elephant with a head butt.

"In very little time he had acquired a most unsavoury reputation. We became pariahs. My mother was distraught by this. Her constitution was weakened and she died from a prolonged attack of hiccups."

Holmes had been paying rapt attention, a curl of smoke arising from the wastebasket where he had emptied his pipe ash while it still glowed. Our visitor continued while I stamped out the conflagration, hopping in pain from the flames as I did so.

"My sister and I were shunned within the village. It was not that the locals hated us, but they feared our stepfather so much that none dare make our acquaintance, for fear it should enrage him."

"That should do it," said I, ignoring my smouldering trousers.

"This is where my sister comes in," she continued after a little hesitation. "Julia is younger than I, or was, I should say."

Here she was overwhelmed by a great wave of sadness.

"She was younger than you?" queried Holmes, oblivious. "Do you mean she's got older since?"

The lady blanched, and grew paler. I stood behind her and drew a finger across my throat and rolled my eyeballs with my tongue sticking out. Holmes' eyes showed that he understood, by which point she had continued.

"My sister was more sociable than I. She was not as willing to accept our status as social outcasts, and while few were prepared to risk the consequences, she did form an attachment with a young man.

"Her affianced was a gentleman of private means, more modest than our own, but then everyone's tends to be. The terms of my mother's will state that our inheritance, which is considerable, reverts from our stepfather's control – we call him Uncle Grintle – to our own upon marriage."

Holmes raised an eyebrow to this.

"Did you stepfather raise any objection to the wedding?"

"Not once, he was in favour of it. The weeks went by in preparation, then a most peculiar thing happened."

"Please be exact as you recount this," urged Holmes.

"That will not be difficult, as the terrible experience is burned into my mind. The main house is large, but the bedrooms are closely connected. The first is my stepfather's, the second was my sister's, and the last is mine. There is no connection between them save the corridor. Do I make myself plain?"

"Not at all, you are most attractive."

She clicked her tongue, presumably a way of thanking Holmes for his handsome compliment.

"The three rooms all look out onto the front garden, and in the summer we often have the windows open. My sister kept hers closed, as she was next to Uncle Grintle, and his habit of smoking strong cigars and performing karaoke through the evening perturbed her.

"One morning I found her ashen. Like myself, she found our stepfather's behaviour most trying. Her hair was turning white, very like mine, and also started falling out in great handfuls.

"She was very distracted, and asked me had I heard a whistling in the night. I replied no, for I am a very sound sleeper. Also, I keep a cat stuffed in each ear to prevent my sleep being disturbed by Uncle Grintle's horrendous snoring.

"Despite this, two days later I was awoken by a horrific scream. Not even the cats could block the sound. I rushed to my sister's room, from where the sound clearly came.

"In the corridor, lying on the floor, was Julia. She was stricken in ways I can hardly bear to think of. Her hands grabbed at the air as though she was drowning, her face blanched with shock. Her eyes rolled hideously in their sockets. Were it not for her one utterance, I would have believed her hysterical."

"What was it she said?"

Miss Simpson looked ahead of her with a deathly stare.

"She said … 'The Speckled Wang, the Speckled Wang!' And then she died."

Our visitor buried her face in her hands, sobbing mightily. I comforted her by putting on my 'Alphonse the Grieving Monkey' hand puppet to assuage her sorrow. Looking at me with astonishment for a moment, she looked about to speak but merely contented herself with throwing the cruet at my balls.

"A fine shot, Miss Simpson," Holmes purred suavely. "Right in the package."

I looked up in some agony and smiled my agreement. Even in moments of extreme discomfort, never let it be said that I do not put our guests at ease.

"Please explain what followed," Holmes continued.

"Upon my father's death, I inherited a significant estate, including a large country house and considerable wealth."

Holmes, who had fainted with greed and delight, came to woozily. From his fallen slump on the chez longe his head lolled forward, a look of great delight on his face.

"It is clear we haven't time to waste, Miss Simpson. Dr. Watson and I will head out to your mansion this very day, complete with our bank books and portable fences."

"Please wait, Mr. Holmes, for I have details so very singular to relate. May I continue?"

"Of course."

"Uncle Grintle is an unusual soul. He was a prospector Far East for much of his career, and attracted a rare number of diseases. It is to these, I am told, that his foul temperament can be attributed."

"He has a consistently violent temper, this uncle?" queried Holmes.

The lady paled.

"Uncle Grintle has his ways, many of which are most peculiar. His habit of opening doors by running at them with full force is particularly irksome, and we have lost two good butlers that way.

"More than that, he possesses a pent up fury that is difficult to describe. The smallest incident can set it off. Why, only yesterday we breakfasted together. All was most pleasant until he detected a spilt crumb on the table. He tore into a furious rage, and was only restrained from assaulting the under-footman by one of the maids, Elsie."

Holmes' focus had been intent, but at this he posed a question.

"She has a winning way about her, this Elsie?"

The young lady paused for a moment.

"Well, she's very good with a mallet. I've had a special maid's uniform run up with a secret hammer pocket in it. Fortunately she was waiting table, and was able to strike him a good one straight on the marbles before too much damage was done."

"And this is far from being an isolated incident?"

"Quite so. We've got through four dining tables, two grandfather clocks and a staircase this month alone."

Holmes brooded for a while. Mrs Hudson brought in coffee, of which our visitor partook while I entertained her by whistling the first movement of Mahler's fifth symphony. I had just got to a particularly difficult string section when Holmes spoke again.

"Fear you for your safety?"

She looked at him as if he were mad.

"Yes, did you think I was here to have my hair cut?"

"Clearly not," Holmes agreed, flashing her the quickest of sharp smiles and hiding his curlers. "Pray continue."

"Uncle Grintle has a long history of eccentricity, in addition to his temper. He keeps most unusual pets, such as a baboon that will insist on performing scenes from Shakespeare's tragedies and a canary trained in the martial arts.

"Our only company is a collection of wandering clue merchants, who roam the countryside obscuring crimes by planting daggers, poison and blood-stained hats everywhere they go."

Holmes held up an imperious hand.

"We have heard enough, Miss Simpson. Head you back home, and the doctor and I will be following directly."

The young lady seemed relieved to be spared further ordeal, and left with great alacrity. Holmes sprang from his chair and rubbed his hands together.

"Get the wheelbarrow and spare clues, Watson. A matter of some note is stirring, for unless I am mistaken, this lady is in grave danger. She is also loaded, so we must move fast."

We rushed directly to the station. As the train pulled out, I reflected on some of Holmes' other adventures, and how his arrival had spelt out the end of one criminal enterprise or another, and sometimes the client as well.

The countryside we passed looked delightful, but Holmes found himself deep in thought. He was looking over some official looking papers, and I had no doubt that he was doing some advance snooping. I left him to it and contended myself with admiring the scenery until we arrived at our destination.

As we neared our destination, the landscape changed markedly. Instead of pleasant cottages, country villages and the like, I saw massive devastation. Frequent lagoons of blood gathered near razed buildings. The despoiled scenery was clearly reeling from ravaging despoilment.

It was clear to me that the recent zombie outbreak had caused massive damage. Many houses were in ruins and we passed the scenes of a number of massacres. Indeed, a good many of England's fine pastoral settings were wrecked by sights of great carnage that spoke of the undead ape infestation's insatiable greed for human flesh.

On several occasions the train was attacked. Luckily, the first time only the ticket inspectors were eaten, which saved us having to pay for the journey. The second time around, we used our window seats to great effect, Holmes using his brain mincer and I my trusty scalpel, which truly came into its own with the close quarters melee opportunities the slightly opened window provided.

A porter rushed through our carriage, shrieking piteously. Evidently a man at his wit's end, he babbled of carnage. The back of the train had been overrun. His best response had been to douse it with kerosene, leap to the next car and set the doomed carriage ablaze before unmooring it.

Calming him as best I could with a hefty thump, I looked to the retreating tracks behind us. Sure enough, from the back of our compartment, the doomed vehicle's fate could be seen. The engulfed timber billowed smoke, a great many writhing beings jostling woefully in the inferno. It was a wretched, damnable sight.

"Glad we didn't travel second class," I commented to Holmes as I resumed my seat.

At the journey's end, we hailed a cab. It was but a short journey to the lady's estate. There were many fine, roaming acres which stretched across three of the Home Counties. An elaborately designed garden, that made Hyde Park look like a window box, greeted our astounded eyes.

It was small wonder that so vast an inheritance may attract foul play. From Holmes' narrowed eyes, it was clear he was thinking the same.

We ascended the stone steps to the great hall, which was a fine example of riches and elegance combined in a most plutocratic way. The pillars flanking the door were of finest marble, and the sign stating that double-glazing was not required was wrought from pure gold.

Feeling our appearance did not quite measure up, Holmes and I paused to change shirts. Sadly our arrival must have been noisier than we realised, as the butler opened the door before we were finished.

"Good afternoon, gentleman," intoned the butler, looking past our semi-attired state without a flutter in his perfect dignity. "I have been advised of your arrival. Would you care to finish dressing and step this way?"

His suave manner was a sharp contrast to our own bumbling arrival. Once the shirts had been buttoned, Holmes and I walked in with as much dignity as we could manage.

If the grandeur of the estate had impressed us, it was nothing to the opulence inside. A vast staircase made of gold dazzled our eyes, so we could hardly see the enormous diamonds used as door handles.

Miss Simpson received us in the drawing room. The butler announced us, sneered quietly and left the room with confident pomposity.

"Ah, Mr. Holmes. Dr. Watson. Welcome to my humble home."

We umm'd and ahh'd at the lowly fixtures, pretending all the while to be accustomed to this rare level of wealth.

An elderly man shuffled into the room, flinching slightly at the sight of us, and settled himself down heftily on a sofa stuffed with cash. Several hundred quid's worth of fivers shot out of the side like a money filled bellows. Holmes' eyes bulged, while I fought the temptation to scoop up great handfuls and run from the room.

The new arrival wore an antiquated uniform; a black blazer with gold epaulettes and a strange hat reminiscent of an admiral.

This, we were informed, was Alderman Wesley, the man the young lady described as her only ally in this dark, wretched matter.

"It is a pleasure to meet you, Alderman."

"You too, Mr. Holmes," said he with the cheeriest of smiles. "And your colleagues, Dr. Watson, of course. You have heard of the matter, I take it?"

"The strange fate that befell Julia Simpson? Yes, and her bizarre statement before her death."

The young lady lowered her eyes. Clearly grief still troubled her, as well it might.

"You must get to the bottom of this mystery, Mr. Holmes. You see, just as her sister complained of hearing whistling shortly before her demise, so has Miss Simpson here recently started to hear whistling at night."

The young lady became animated at this point.

"You both remember me saying that I stuff a cat into each ear to prevent my sleep being disturbed? Recently I have stopped doing this, as my ears have developed fleas."

She stopped to scratch at this point, and a small insect leaped from the side of her head. It was less than a charming accompaniment to her youth and good looks.

"Julia complained of hearing whistling through the night just before she died." She stifled a sob and looked to the side, bravely conquering tears.

"I can only feel, Mr. Holmes – I fear the worst, and that my days are numbered. Perhaps I too will fall victim to the Speckled Wang."

I began wondering what this cryptic horror might be, and certainly Holmes looked more puzzled than I have ever seen him, which is saying something.

"This was shortly after we announced our engagement," the Alderman told us. "Miss Simpson had done me the honour of accepting my proposal of marriage. I know there is a massive age difference, but I can overlook the odd grey hair," he told us with no little munificence.

"It was at this point that the young lady asked me to stay here, to see what horrors lay afoot. It was a mutual decision, taken by her. Naturally I was eager to do all I can to avoid a tragedy, but I'm blessed, Mr. Holmes, if I know what I should do."

Holmes looked reflective, resting his hands on his lap. His head leaned to one side, eyelids half shut as the thoughts progressed, his long thin fingers interlaced in a study of intense thought.

When he opened his eyes fully, he looked at Miss Simpson with the full force of his intellect. She, barely noticing, gave a wan smile.

"The first thing is to show me the rooms in question, first your sister's, and then your own. I need to determine the common ground, if any."

"But of course, Mr. Holmes."

"I should like to be shown around the house by the butler and on my own, if that is agreeable to you. I realise this is something of an odd request, but I need to see the ground here with a clear, impartial eye."

"Of course, Mr. Holmes. Dr. Watson, will you join us in some refreshment?"

I assented with hearty vigour, as the journey had been a long one. I was shown into a dining room of some enormity, where I was shocked to find a great many wild animals grazing next to the tea service.

"These belong to my stepfather, Uncle Grintle. You recall my mentioning him? He acquired a taste for exotic creatures while in Calcutta, and has indulged this enthusiasm in no uncertain terms."

"I see," I replied, offering a passing zebra a cucumber sandwich. "Could not one of these animals have produced the whistling that has so disturbed you?"

"I have never heard any of them make any kind of music. Unless the animals want to form a band, of course. But that would be daft."

I agreed. It's well known that wild animals have great difficulty keeping time and rarely, if ever, get any gigs. As if to prove me wrong, four chinchillas immediately struck up a medley of popular songs, ending in the always moving "Dolly's Showing Her Ankles," one of the racier songs of our time.

I found myself applauding thoroughly, and throwing muffins to the entertaining and surprisingly tuneful creatures, who accepted the foodstuffs with good grace.

Miss Simpson attempted to share my enjoyment of the matter, but unsurprisingly the enormous weight of the fearsome situation wore her down.

I consoled her as best I could, assuring her of Holmes' reputation and brilliance. Resisting the temptation to snigger here and there, she accepted my solace with some relief.

"When do you imagine Mr. Holmes will have something to report?"

I pondered.

"It is hard to say." Inwardly I rolled my eyes and trotted out the spiel. "He extracts as much information from the scene as possible. His precise nature is sometimes a test of patience."

"I see," she commented.

To fill the time, she showed me around the collection of family portraits which adorned the walls. Her ancestors were all painted by some of the famous artists of the day, and a gruesome collection of ugly delinquents they were, too.

As we talked, Miss Simpson glided effortlessly into sophistication, and I endeavoured to make high society talk.

"Have you seen the new production of *La Traviata* at Covent Garden?" she asked.

"No. Verdi makes me constipated."

One of the portraits grabbed my attention. As I was discussing this, I pointed out a feature of the painting. My finger accidentally touched the frame, which receded slightly into the wall. A deep set mechanical whirring could be heard, and a hidden door opened.

"There's a secret passage here," I exclaimed in amazement.

"Yes, the séance room." She lead me through, bewildered as I was at the recent development and her reaction, as though this were utterly natural.

It was a long corridor, hewed out of stone, with trickles of water flowing over the rough cut rock. The dank atmosphere reeked of decay. It was like smelling a tomb's breath. Even the somewhat effete bell push, hewn from granite, held a faintly sinister air.

At the end was a room that glowed with an unnatural light. In fact, I fancied I could hear sinister organ music that got louder with every step. As soon as I stepped in, I saw that it was indeed a mire of hellish iniquity.

The grisly, doom laden air seemed to strange the life from me, so oppressive was the atmosphere. Skulls drizzled with blood were stacked across shelves made of bones. A barely recognisable human cadaver sat festering in the corner.

"Good God!"

"Yes, we are thinking of decorating in here," Miss Simpson informed me brightly.

Necromantic slogans had been daubed on the walls in thick red gore. Some of these were faded, charred in appearance and grainy.

"What happened here?" I asked.

"That bit there was written in black pudding, as Uncle Grintle had run out of fresh."

"What in the name of all things holy does he get up to in here?"

"He picked up all manner of dark practices when he was at school, where he studied voodoo because he was no good at trigonometry.

"It was a practice I chanced across as a child. He was surrounded by candles, his eyes rolled fully back in his head so only the whites were visible. A low, unearthly chant left his mouth like a vile spirit being released."

"Such a fearful ordeal," I could only imagine the terror it must have inspired. "What did you do?"

"Oh, I left him to it and started lunch without him," she said in a matter of fact way, as though discussing a game of cards rather than a diabolic pact.

"You appear to have handled the matter with the most striking grace," I could only pay tribute.

"Uncle Grintle is a rare and vicious soul. He comes from a family with a long tradition of being violent lunatics." This made me think of Holmes, one of whose relatives claimed to have invented the twig, and was known to run through forests demanding royalties.

"His real name is Vespasian Scintoro Noblet," she continued. "He changed it to Grintle Roycott because he didn't want to be conspicuous."

I pulled the Twattometer from my pocket, switched it on and repeated both names. Unsurprisingly, it hummed loudly into life.

"I thought as much."

We left the séance room and returned to the portrait gallery.

"I do hope Mr. Holmes has something to report soon, for I am on tenterhooks."

"Here he comes now."

The butler walked towards us, my celebrated colleague following in his wake. Holmes' bracing lack of courtesy had evidently been in play, for the butler wore an air of unmistakeable irritation.

"I regret, Mr. Holmes, that I cannot vouchsafe to you the combination of the safe," the butler was saying to the clearly disgruntled detective. Upon seeing us, Holmes' expression changed from consternation to concern.

"Watson, what has occurred? You look like you've just had a shock."

I told him of the matter of the bizarre room. He listened seriously.

"Miss Simpson," he intoned gravely, looking her square in the face. "There is a larger matter to hand, bigger than even the murder of your sister and your own impending death." I rolled my eyes, for his lack of tact was, at times, a monumental pisser. He continued, "There is a plague of unnatural mutations. The dead live again as winged monkey savages. Our whole way of life is threatened."

"Oh," she replied faintly. "Does that mean I should cancel the wedding?"

"It means you must tell me everything," Holmes insisted.

"Uncle Grintle worked for the government, helping them raise the dead. I gather he was expecting to make a great deal of money, although shortly before my sister died, he complained bitterly. He said he'd been betrayed, but that he would have the last laugh."

Holmes pondered for a moment.

"Do you see the connection?"

"I do indeed," I replied with no little excitement.

"Quite," agreed Holmes. "Using this skill, I can resurrect all the clients who've died under my protection, and make them pay their bills. Superb."

He was delighted, rubbing his hands together with glee the way he does whenever he thinks money is forthcoming. I struck my forehead, lamenting the calluses I have developed there since beginning my association with Holmes. Miss Simpson continued before I could speak, however.

"I think he made some kind of pact with the Devil. Or it may have been the local council, I'm not sure which."

"Easily confused," I admitted.

"Why, does that throw any light on the situation?" she asked in wide eyed innocence. "I have no idea what this could relate to, or of the importance of him raising the dead. I thought it was a blessing for him to have a hobby."

"Good news, Miss Simpson. I can shed some light on the matter."

Before she could reply, a great bellow met our ears. Startled animals ran amok in primal terror as the sound of a great predator met our ears. I have heard a great many terrible noises in my time, many of them coming from Holmes' violin, but this was worse than any of them.

We turned to see a man of huge build and the reddest face I've ever seen. He was charging like a man who meant business. Very clearly this was Grintle Roycott, of unsavoury reputation. Seeing him in person demonstrated the accuracy of Miss Simpson's remarks about his vicious nature. Indeed, the rage on his face was so intense I could only wonder what Holmes had been doing. Had he been so rash as to provoke this maddened giant directly?

Before the situation could come to light, the smouldering Roycott plucked a grandfather clock from the side of the room as though it weighed no more than a matchstick. Swatting it from side to side like a tennis racket, he advanced on us with no little alacrity.

We departed the mansion with some speed as our client's ferocious uncle chased us out. He was waving his chosen weapon like a riding crop, doing his damnedest to reduce characters in the world of detective fiction to the tune of two.

We regained both breath and composure outside, while the miracle of yet another close shave worked its way through our systems.

Pausing a moment to consult the pint of liquid deduction I keep in my coat, Holmes gargled a few quick measures of nerve restorer and faced me with a powerful shudder.

"This case, Watson, may be the end of us."

"Quite," I agreed, returning the life saver to my grasp and sinking a quick draft of equilibrium. "The way that devil plucked a heavy ornament from the ground as though it were a pencil, and swung it like he meant business made me shudder."

"We must not let it deter us in our quest for the truth," Holmes said with a wink as we slunk away, hiccupping slightly. We spent the next several hours considering our best approach, draining my flask as we did so. The zombies were gathered at the far end of the grounds, if the distant snuffling noises were anything to go by.

Night was falling before we decided to make a move. Holmes was decamoflaging himself, plucking twigs from his Deerstalker and taking the teapot off his magnifying glass.

Pausing for a moment to water the plants, I noticed a grimy individual approaching us. The distinctive sound of a throat being cleared met my ears.

"If I could have a moment, gentlemen."

Holmes' vast observational ability had missed the new arrival. His leapt several inches into the air and he let go of a cry of alarm that echoed through the gardens.

We crouched down as the "ucking ell ucking ell ucking ell" sounds reverberated away. I looked at my colleague with a certain measure of contempt. He looked sheepish as the new arrival began to speak.

"Pardon me for interrupting, Mr. Holmes. I know your time is valuable and I am only a humble servant," began our respectful interlocutor. He was a small, elderly man looking curiously at Holmes.

"There he goes, pissed again!"

"There's been devilry afoot," he informed us with no little excitement. "For while the ladies of the house have always been kind souls, Mr. Roycott is a demon incarnate, make no mistake. There are many dark deeds going on at the hall."

"Tell us more," Holmes looked intrigued. The man moved closer to us, his eyes peering wildly from side to side.

"The old house used to be such a friendly place, until he came here. It all changed. Some nights the air filled with razored lightning. Strange curses rocked the surroundings while he and his terrible helpers worked. When I found out that he needed dead bodies ..." His voice tapered off.

"Mean you these nefarious fellows brought Roycott corpses for his foul work?"

"After a fashion, sir, yes. They kidnapped locals, and in the dead of night would bring them to the house. Dr. Roycott, evil man that he is, delighted in it. They were slaughtered right in front of him."

The depths of this diabolic troll's malignant spirit astounded me.

"What was his reaction?"

"He laughed and heaped praise on them, calling them his perfect minions. They liked it, but they left before he began his strange, unnatural rituals. These fellows are thugs, killers. Rough, low brutes, but the unnatural air of necromancy frightened them."

Holmes' nostrils twitched.

"How do you know this?"

"I used to sleep in the stable, for my unusual smell bothered the ladies of the house. The noises of Roycott's terrible pair of assistants woke me one night. From then on I made a point of keeping my eye on the matter. As such, I have seen a large number of unusual things going on during the night, including many secret murders."

"Do you know who the accomplices where?"

"Oh yes," he replied, and Holmes rubbed his hands together with glee. "It was it was the work of none other than the Dobb Street Nutters. I recognised them from the newspapers."

There was an intake of shock from Holmes.

"I know the very gang," Holmes spluttered. "They are one of the vilest, most cut throat gang of robbers I ever encountered."

"As bad as that?" I queried, taken aback by Holmes' reaction.

"They are the very dregs, Watson. Worse than the Harley Street Razor Physicians of dreaded repute, who carry out surgery on unsuspecting passers-by and then steal their wallets. If this pack of brutes are the quarry, then this is indeed a dangerous hunt."

Holmes fingered his chin for a moment, an expression of concern on his face.

"I assume Miss Simpson knows nothing of these killings?"

"No, for she is the mildest of souls. I am sure that she knows nothing of them. It was the raising of the dead that worried me, though. The corpses would come back to life, often complaining about having a stiff neck or some such, as though they had just awoken from a long sleep."

The crack of gunfire rousted our attention. The high pitched screeches of panicked apes mingled with bloodthirsty laughter. It had our attention immediately as dozens of the creatures raced out of the woods as though in terrible panic.

"That'll be Dr. Roycott now. He enjoys spending the evenings slaughtering. He says it reminds him of practising medicine. A large cluster of these bizarre flying creatures, the end product of his experiments, gathers in the woodland."

With a glance to each other, Holmes and I resolved to retire from the strange environs of Stoke Roycott, apprehend the accomplices then return.

Surprisingly, we found ourselves able to return to London within a single sentence. At our Baker Street lodgings, Holmes urged me to find my darkest clothes and a stout stick as well as my gun.

"We take no chances with these devils," he instructed. "The slightest mistake could be calamitous."

"Think you we can apprehend them tonight?"

When Holmes is fraught in the middle of a case, his manner assumes an intensity that is rarely seen elsewhere. His eyes glinted with inner steel and a burning desire for justice – and money – spurred him on.

We paused briefly to telegram Scotland Yard for the current timetable of crimes scheduled for that evening.

"I'll never know why they don't use that to catch the blighters themselves," Holmes commented to me as we awaited the reply. "It would net them a far greater share of criminal London.

However, the mind of the average police inspector is decidedly odd. Ah, here is the reply now."

Quickly scanning the response, we set out to hail a cab. Our destination was a dimly lit side street near the Bunton Road jewellers, a lucrative expanse of the finest gems the Empire has to offer. If Holmes' information was correct – and Lord knows, it usually wasn't – this richly stocked merchant was about to be robbed by our gang.

We alighted several streets away, so as not to alert wrong doers to our presence.

"See you then, Mr Holmes," called the hansom driver, chuckling richly to himself at my colleague's expression of severe miffedness. Contenting himself by saluting the disappearing cab with two fingers, he then plucked at my elbow and directed me down a side street.

It was the kind of locale that suggests crime. Thick swirls of fog hung dense in the air while stark yellow streaks of gaslight were smothered by gloom. Even the cobblestones seemed to ring with vice as we walked over them.

"Hist, Watson, for our prey approaches." We squashed ourselves into a doorway and crouched out of the light.

Their arrival was heralded by a low, furtive muttering. Heavy footsteps made their way closer. It was clear we were dealing with nefarious types as they were wearing masks and carrying hammers.

"Respectable people don't go out like that," I hissed to Holmes. He shot me a thumbs up while I, proud of my developing observational skills, resumed our vigil.

As soon as they got close enough to where we hid, Holmes and I leapt from the shadows. We both brandished our revolvers and made with our best 'hit the dirt' faces.

"Allow me to introduce the Dobb Street Nutters: One Buttock Harris and his light-fingered friend, Three Cheeks McGuire," Holmes intoned with no little pride in his voice.

In the murk of the evening, their faces became masked leers of hatred. Three Cheeks Maguire was closest to us. Sat upon his ignoble head was a battered top hat, one that had clearly seen its share of hard living. I took this for pretensions or possibly a tribute to his criminal master.

One Buttock Harris had less of a sinister edge. With his gormless grin, vacant expression and gold fob watch, he looked like a professional moron. His clothing was pristine and expensive. It was only when we locked eyes that I realised there was something of the dangerous animal lurking in his soul.

Holmes cocked his revolver and called to them.

"You thought you could outwit Sherlock Holmes?" my colleague taunted.

"Yes," they replied, quite reasonably. "If it weren't for that damn schedule of crimes, we would've done, too."

"That's enough of that," Holmes moved on quickly. "In return for leniency, tell me all about Dr. Grintle Roycott and his heinous schemes."

After some cursing, the unsavoury due came clean. They had supplied him with funds for his strange animal habit and grandfather clock smashing habit. It transpired that, while his daughters were both loaded, he was of extremely humble means, and had acquired tastes far beyond them.

"What of Miss Simpson's fate? What know you of that?"

"We know nothing," replied One Buttock Harris insistently. "Apart from the fact he's going to kill her tomorrow evening."

"Aha! And how?"

"Of that we know nothing," stated Three Cheeks McGuire. "He'll be using the Speckled Wang again, no doubt," he commented to his accomplice. "But I have no idea what it is."

"I see. Watson, get the large criminal net. We need to act swiftly."

Three Cheeks Maguire had a ruddy, knave's face. His mirthless smile, framed by flushed and ruddy cheeks, told us he wasn't going quietly. Malice sparkled in his eyes. I could see that, even though we were armed, this was going to be a struggle.

A quiet fluttering of wings drifted over our heads. For a distracted second I thought perhaps the pigeons were getting larger, then reality crushed its way home. Four of the brutes landed, the largest ape bearing its teeth with a horrific, ravenous bellow.

They lumbered towards us, their eyes dead. There was a menacing, insistent shuffle to their step. Holmes and I were ready for the terrible, brain hungry foe. Umbrellas at the ready, we deflected the fiends away from us. The disliked of water repelled them, and this meant they retreated straight into the unsavoury duo we had been about to apprehend.

It is rare to see villains get their just desserts. These two were dealt with in a particularly gruesome fashion. Three Cheeks Maguire died first. A zombie punched through the roof of his top hat, cracked his skull and pulled out the tasty grey matter within, drooling slightly over the rim of his butchered topper.

As Maguire squealed like a pig being turned into a sandwich, One Buttock Harris tried to defend himself. Being a man with a certain primitive savagery, he braced himself for the attack. Swinging at the nearest creature, his knife connected with the beast's rib.

Its howl of pain brought renewed savagery from the rest of the pack. The others plucked Maguire's limbs from his torso like diners eating chicken at a picnic. His armless, legless body fell to the floor with a splat. He looked about him with outrage.

He was allowed about a second of futile gnashing, rage clearly gushing into his primordial features. The apes then tore him apart, not even bothering to eat him. It was a hideous, grisly spectacle, but to be honest I quite enjoyed seeing the two vicious rogues getting their comeuppance.

Holmes turned to me, his face white with shock.

"We must hie us back to Stoke Roycott and get this matter wrapped up before the story ends." He reflected for a minute. "There is one more thing to be dealt with first."

"What's that?" I enquired.

"Last orders," said he with a wise expression.

I realised there and then that I was in the presence of a rare intellect indeed. There are times when Holmes' reputation is well founded, and the groundings for his fame secure.

The following day began rare and early. I wasn't there to see it, owing to a late night, but I assume dawn was first thing in the morning. It usually is.

We breakfasted with the intensity of two men with a rare and challenging task before them. Holmes was silent and, but for the occasional relighting of his pipe, motionless. I munched toast with the determination of a man of action, and wiped marmalade from my shirt with the cool, steely determination of a hunter.

These pre-case resolution breakfasts require a high level of intrigue. Mrs. Hudson brought in the coffee with the air of a commando staking out a target, and the boiled eggs were consumed after the fashion of a high level military engagement.

As we repeated our journey of yesterday, a grim silence descended. Holmes is a beacon of intense, private thought at such times. When the life of a client is in the balance his countenance becomes near subterranean, such is his focus, knowing that the slightest misstep on his part could mean having nobody to pay the bill.

As there were no hansom cabs available at the station, we hailed a couple of passing minor characters and persuaded them to carry us the long, sinister way to Grintle Towers. The dastardly plans of our nemesis were fresh in my mind as I considered his vicious conduct.

Certainly this was an opponent of great danger. I regretted not having checked the sporting goods stores of London to see if any of them sold grandfather clock proof helmets, but this was no time for regret. We would have to be resolute. I would shoot at the slightest opportunity.

Holmes had telegraphed ahead, appraising Miss Simpson of the danger and of our arrival. She had agreed to arranged for us to be met in the grounds. This would avoid the fearsome wrath of her stepfather, the better for us to prepare for the evening's plot resolution.

Alderman Wesley greeted us some distance from the house. Such was the need for stealth that he was in camouflage. As we approached him, I could saw this would have been more effective had he not been stood upright in a freshly mown field and wearing a petunia on his head, but it was not the time to mention that.

"Mr Holmes," he began, his manner bearing no little agitation. "Have you good news of the Speckled Wang?"

"I am prepared to say that soon this vicious business will be concluded. Apart from that, I must ask that you trust me."

"I shall indeed," assented he. "I gather matters are progressing in this grim affair?"

"Assuredly so. This is no idle speculation, Alderman, but a cold fact: unless action is taken, your fiancé will not live to see the morning."

"She doesn't like mornings, being a late riser, but I take the point," mused the good fellow wisely. "Better to be alive and have the option."

"Quite," affirmed Holmes. "We must tread carefully, for our foe in this matter is a cunning, brutal fellow of great strength and a dastardly mind."

"I agree, he does have a basardly mind," mused the good fellow, mishearing slightly. "I saw him punch out a baboon yesterday for messing up a speech from *King Lear*."

"Yes, they do tend to confuse the imagery. Theatre notwithstanding, there is a need to act swiftly and with guile, for unless action is taken, a terrible fate awaits Miss Simpson."

"I would have hoped our marriage would be a good thing," replied the Alderman with a touch of hauteur. "It's not as though anyone asked you."

"I refer not to your forthcoming nuptials, which I am confident will be delightful," Holmes appeased smoothly. "I refer to an attempt on her life, to be made this very evening. Have you arranged everything I asked for?"

"Certainly," confirmed he. "There is a side entrance you may use to enter the house unseen, but I think this will be unnecessary. Grintle Roycott is asleep, and your arrival should go unreported, for none of the staff will even approach him, due to his temper."

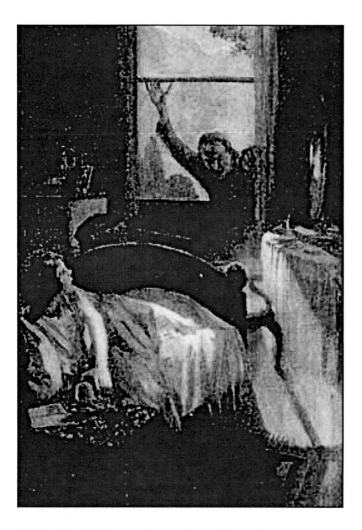

Mabel decided to put a lock on Henry's trousers.

"Even so, every precaution must be observed, for there may be a grave many criminal elements attached to this. We will take our positions now, and I shall tell you what I need to be done."

We made our way to Grintle Towers, once more awed by the immense show of wealth the house afforded. Holmes enquired after Elsie, the maid whose nimble habits with a mallet had more than once dissuaded our quarry from his destructive path.

"Sadly she is in London, attending upon a elderly relative who is at death's door and has yet to make a will. It is an inconvenience, I confess, for her intervention has guaranteed safety on more than one occasion."

A pity," commented Holmes, "but no matter, for Dr. Watson and I shall be in attendance. I will need for you, Alderman, to trust us entirely in this matter and tell no-one of our plans."

With that he related our plan of action for the evening. The honest gentleman's expression turned to one of horror, but Holmes persuaded him that this was indeed necessary, and the only course that could see justice prevail over murder.

Put like that, it did seem like one hell of an ending was on the way.

Evening crawled in. Apprehension was toying with my nerves and making me start at trifles. It made sitting through dessert difficult, but that could not be helped.

Miss Simpson had been most appreciative of Holmes' concern. She fully accepted that the dangerous ordeal ahead of her was necessary, and adjusted to the situation with commendable resolve.

Later that night, Holmes and I were positioned against the window of her room. Knowing that her sister's death stemmed from some dread event that occurred as she slept, it was imperative we did not make ourselves known until the moment was right.

Admittedly, in hindsight, sitting down to dinner with Grintle Roycott at the main table had been something of a blunder. Neither Holmes nor myself are particularly fond of sandwiches, so it could not be helped. Besides, he was completely engaged in forging a will, so it seems unlikely our presence was detected.

Stood still behind the curtain, I marvelled at how loud tiny sounds appear when one is engaged on a mission of stealth. My nervous fingers rechecked my revolver. Once more I stared out into the vast lands surrounding the house where, from some unseen position, great peril would come.

We had been in position for perhaps two hours when Holmes sharpened my attention with a nudge. I tensed, and sure enough a thin, high-pitched whistle could be heard. Realising this was the same sound that heralded Julia Simpson's death, it was

140

clear that matters were swiftly approaching a dangerous conclusion.

Holmes moved silently into the darkened room, where his client was sleeping soundly, having imbibed several bottles of wine to assist her in this tense matter. A sliding noise met our ears, a menacing slither of danger approaching our slumbering client.

Suddenly, Holmes lashed out. He had brought a cudgel with him, and using this he repeatedly hit at some unseen figure in the dark.

As the villain struck, Holmes realised most of his hula hoop had been stolen.

A cry of pain and enraged distress broke out. I rushed from my position, pistol at the ready. A deranged animal snarl growled out from the dark.

"Now, Watson. Fire!"

I dispensed several shots in the direction of the noise, hoping as I did so that a bullet might graze Holmes. Nothing serious, of course, but one gets these whims.

The fall of a body could be heard. Holmes raised the light from the gas lantern, that the room could better be seen.

Lying on the floor, horribly wounded and arching with death throes, was the naked figure of Dr. Grintle Roycott.

"Behold, Watson. The Speckled Wang."

I looked down. Sure enough, a bright patina of unhealthy looking spots could be seen upon the fallen man. In fact, they were right on the old chap. It was clear enough what the eponymous mystery had been. A bottle of poison lay at his feet.

"Oh, Mr. Holmes, Mr. Holmes! What means this bizarre scene?"

Our client had stirred from her intoxicated sleep, as gunfire in the bedroom does tend to disturb rest. The celebrated sleuth was courtesy itself in his attentions, soothing her with assurances that the matter was concluded and that his fees should be settled within twenty-eight days.

Some hours later, the local police arrived and the village doctor pronounced Grintle Roycott dead. I would have done so myself, but it seemed a little pointless, as he was lying motionless and full of bullets.

"I do not understand," lamented Miss Simpson. "What happened?"

"Your stepfather, the fiend, was a man of greed and dissolution." Holmes pronounced. "Upon learning of your sister's marriage, and realising how this would affect his own finances, he took pains to prevent the match.

"Having worked as a doctor in the Far East, he had acquired a vast knowledge of rare poisons, many of which are all but unheard of on these shores. It was one of these that claimed your sister's life and, had we not intervened, would have taken your own.

"I checked his service with the medical brigade on Harley Street, and found that he had been a keen hunter whilst in Calcutta.

"Being a man of primitive habits, he had been in the practice of stalking his prey in the nude, which I am told brings one closer to the Neanderthal. I refer you to a clue, which I found in Roycott's study the first time I visited your home."

Holmes passed over a piece of paper.

I want to be a caveman, it read.

"This in mind, he felt nudity was the correct practice. Such was the state of his corrupted, primitive mind, he could regard his own stepdaughters as quarry. This, I fear, was the degraded character of Grintle Roycott."

"But the sound, what was that whistle?"

"Despite his savage inclinations, he was still an Englishman at heart. When preparing for the hunt by disrobing, he naturally whistled as he beheld the colourful souvenirs a tropical disease had left on his chopper."

"Beg pardon?" our puzzled client asked for clarification.

"The nobrot still dismayed him."

"The Speckled Wang!" cried Miss Simpson.

"Quite so," confirmed Holmes, "but I think everyone's realised that by now."

Outside, we could hear the police officers battling it out with the army of undead apes that buzzed them overhead, picking off the occasional constable. I could hear a number of gunshots mixing with cries of dismay as officers saw their colleagues fall.

"Such a terrible blight upon the country," I observed sadly.

"At least we got the man who helped this madness come to pass."

"Sad to say his work will live after him," mused Holmes. "The rule of our country now given over to resurrected, brain chewing, flying apes."

"True," I agreed. "I wonder if anyone will notice?"

"You call that a plot?"

Sherlock Holmes and the Underpants of Death

Legendary detective Sherlock Holmes is a byword for intelligence and efficiency. Not anymore. Detailing some of his less famous exploits, including the infamous drive by shittings of 1894, this rare volume covers a side of Holmes scarcely seen by the public: the real one.

Only this collection reveals the mystery of the lingering stench, how Professor Moriarty didn't die and the truth behind the sinister Underpants of Death, a tale to freeze the blood and rapidly unblock the colon.

Also available from LDB Publishing

The Ingredients Of A Good Thriller

Ever wanted to write a thriller?

Ever thought you had a story but didn't know where to start?

This book gives you:

- A detailed breakdown of characters.
- Tips on getting the reader's attention.
- Ways of effectively telling stories.
- The impact of good dialogue.
- Explorations of top thrillers.
- Hints on how to give your story impact.

The Ingredients Of A Good Thriller is a guide to an area that has huge potential and gives great pleasure. It's an easy to follow approach to writing and improving your story. It provides solid examples to show you what works - and what doesn't.

Clear and easy to follow, this book is helpful for any thriller writer. Don't start without it!

Lightning Source UK Ltd.
Milton Keynes UK
UKOW041919071212

203344UK00002B/312/P